KNOW YOUR FAITH

To Larry & Roberta:

In Christian

fellowship

John Pope

Eph 1:2

KNOW YOUR FAITH

In a Decade of Evangelism

John Young

HODDER & STOUGHTON
LONDON   SYDNEY   AUCKLAND

British Library Cataloguing in Publication Data
A record for this book is available from the British Library

ISBN 0 340 54487 2

Printed and bound in Great Britain by
Cox & Wyman Ltd, Reading, Berkshire

Hodder and Stoughton
A division of Hodder Headline PLC
338 Euston Road
London NW1 3BH

Dedication

— to Linda and Joy and all who hold the faith in very tough circumstances.

— to Elsie and Christopher and all who hold the faith in simplicity.

— to Michael and Christine and all who struggle for faith.

— to Jean and Margaret and all who have lost their faith.

— to John and Chris and all who make it easy for others to believe in God.

* * *

Euangelio (that we cal gospel) is a greke worde, and signyfyth good, mery, glad and joyfull tydings, that maketh a mannes hert glad, and maketh hym synge, daunce and leepe for joye.

(William Tyndale: 1494?–1536)

* * *

May we who share Christ's body live his risen life; we who drink his cup bring life to others; we whom the Spirit lights give light to the world. Keep us firm in the hope you have set before us . . .

(The Alternative Service Book 1980)

Contents

* * *

Each chapter is divided into six sections:
  Getting started
  Setting it out
  Probing the meaning
  Questions
  Viewpoints
  Meditation and Prayer

Acknowledgements

My warmest thanks to Margaret Drake-Jones and Barbara Thompson for typing many drafts. In addition to this practical help I needed advice on many points. I received it abundantly from Margaret and from Christopher Idle, David Makepeace, Linda Norman, Annette Plaxton and Chris Woodcock. I am more grateful than I can say for their encouragement, friendship and sound judgement. It has been a privilege to work with three editors, and I am glad to record my indebtedness to Carolyn Armitage, Juliet Newport and Christine Plunkett for constructive comments, cheerful encouragement and time-consuming attention to detail. My thanks too to John Martin, Editor of the *Church of England Newspaper*, who rang one afternoon and suggested a Study Guide based on the Apostles' Creed . . .

I am grateful to St Paul's Church, York, for the Questionnaire on page 70.

The Vicar was old and very devout, but sometimes far away during the Services. One Sunday, as the Creed was reached, there was silence. So the Curate went across, touched his arm gently and prompted, 'I believe in God, Vicar'. 'So do I', replied the old man happily, 'So do I'. (Source: Christ Church, Virginia Water — whose Vicar it isn't!)

Foreword

I think it was Frank Chadwick, a former Bishop of Barking, who coined the phrase 'custard-pie evangelism'. I knew instinctively what he meant; the unthinking and sometimes aggressive application of a pre-packaged gospel to everyone who comes within range. The launch of the Decade of Evangelism has given rise to fears (unjustified in my view) that we shall see more of this kind of gospel presentation. But it does not have to be like that; there are far more effective ways to bring people to Christ.

One such way is through discussion or study groups, in which the members are helped to learn honestly. There is no heavy introduction, no attempt at indoctrination. Instead the group combines explanation with discovery. It is this kind of group for whom the chapters of John Young's book are designed. The author is a gifted communicator and a convincing apologist for the evangelical faith. But he soft-pedals his approach, without however concealing his opinions, so as to allow his readers to come to their own conclusions. For him it is more important that they think and decide for themselves than that they meekly subscribe to a given party line.

One thing is for sure. Anyone who sits in on a group which follows these eight investigations into the Apostles' Creed (or, better still, spends sixteen sessions on them, for they contain so much good material) will end up as a more informed and more intelligent Christian than when they began. And if that is not effective evangelism, I don't know what is.

So I welcome the opportunity given me by John Young and his publisher to commend this excellent study guide to all parishes who in this decade want to use the oblique approach to evangelism in order to bring people nearer to a saving faith in Christ. I hope it will be well used. I am sure it will be greatly valued by all who make the effort.

The Rt Rev John Taylor,
Bishop of St Albans
New Year's Day 1991

Introduction

THE APOSTLES' CREED

I believe in God, the Father almighty,
   creator of heaven and earth.
I believe in Jesus Christ, his only Son, our Lord.
He was conceived by the power of the Holy Spirit
and born of the Virgin Mary.
He suffered under Pontius Pilate,
was crucified, died, and was buried.
He descended to the dead.
On the third day he rose again.
He ascended into heaven,
and is seated at the right hand of the Father.
He will come again to judge the living and the dead.
I believe in the Holy Spirit,
the holy catholic Church,
the communion of saints,
the forgiveness of sins,
the resurrection of the body,
and the life everlasting. Amen.

(ASB: 1980)

I believe in God the Father Almighty, maker of heaven and earth:

And in Jesus Christ his only Son our Lord, Who was conceived by the Holy Ghost, Born of the Virgin Mary, Suffered under Pontius Pilate, Was crucified, dead, and buried: He descended into hell; The third day he rose again from the dead; He ascended into heaven, And sitteth on the right hand of God the

Father Almighty; From thence he shall come to judge the quick and the dead.

I believe in the Holy Ghost; The holy Catholick Church; The Communion of Saints; The Forgiveness of sins; The Resurrection of the body, And the life everlasting. Amen. (Book of Common Prayer: 1662)

HISTORICAL NOTE

In one sense the Apostles' Creed is not the Apostles' Creed at all. At no point did the early followers of Jesus get together to draw up and issue a formal statement of basic Christian beliefs. The Creed as we know it (give or take a few phrases) emerged during the fourth century – based on affirmations of faith made by candidates for baptism. But in another sense the title 'Apostles' Creed' is accurate; for every point of the Creed is based upon the teaching of the Apostles as outlined in the New Testament.

NOTE TO FREE CHURCH CHRISTIANS

The Creeds are used regularly in Anglican, Catholic and Orthodox Churches. They are said less frequently in most Free Churches – and by some, not at all.

It would be a mistake to think that these ancient Creeds somehow 'belong' to those Churches which say them week-by-week. They are the heritage of *all* believers. These words were quarried – often in turbulent circumstances – by Christians of earlier generations who had four vital aims:

a) A desire to uphold the teaching of the Bible.
b) A desire to state their faith in terms which could be understood in their own times.

c) A concern to combat error.

d) A desire to listen to God's Spirit – who, according to the promise of Jesus, will guide his disciples 'into all truth' (John 16:13).

These aims hold good for us. The historic Creeds are important pointers as we seek to understand and share our faith.

PLEASE READ THESE INTRODUCTORY NOTES

'Evidence of widespread ignorance of the Christian faith among Church-goers is massive and alarming' (Archbishop John Habgood).

These eight chapters are written with those words in mind. They are intended to engage with key aspects of the Christian faith – particularly important as many churches embark on a Decade of Evangelism. These pages are designed for two kinds of readers:

First, they are intended for the individual reader – for those who want to apply their minds to the basics of the Christian faith in the time-honoured way, with a book on lap or pillow (I sadly confess that reading in bed is a gymnastic feat which has always eluded me; but I understand that others have more success). I hope that the solo reader will find *Know Your Faith* helpful and readable.

But it is intended for group study too. Three hundred Christians tackled an early draft of the course on a trial run basis. I am grateful to Anglicans, Baptists, Catholics, Methodists, and Quakers in North Yorkshire's Ryedale for their helpful comments and enthusiastic encouragement. Many other groups followed the course in the summer of 1991 when these chapters were serialised and carried as inserts in the *Church of England Newspaper*.

What this book is not:

(a) This book is *not an historical study* of the Apostles' Creed.

You will find a historical note on Page 12 but this course is aimed at the 1990s. Our concern is with the modern world, e.g:

- What does it mean to believe in God the Father Almighty *today*?
- What is the significance of the Holy Spirit for us *now*?

(b) This book is *not an exhaustive study*.

Eight weeks is quite long enough for a study course, so I have made some bold links and a few omissions. Most of the topics covered by the Apostles' Creed have been touched upon but I have, of necessity, been selective within each subject. Decisions about which aspects to include/exclude have been difficult. For example, in the chapter entitled 'I Believe in Jesus Christ', I have addressed the phrase 'Born of the Virgin Mary' – a question often discussed in the modern Church. But this means that some other aspects of belief in Jesus Christ as Saviour and Lord have not been addressed as fully as some might wish.

You will not find a complete theology of the New Testament here; you will encounter many crucial issues.

What this book is:

In many ways this is an ordinary book – but not quite. It is a study course. Several pages carry information. Most of this writing is my own, but not all Christians see the issues raised in the same light, and every chapter contains a variety of viewpoints. You will find plenty to chew on, agree with, argue with and think about. This book is a springboard; it is incomplete until you have 'written' your section. So the single most important section in each chapter is the list of wide-ranging *Questions* for individuals to ponder and groups to discuss. Each chapter will end, not with *my* last word, but with *yours*.

By including a range of *Viewpoints* – some of which I disagree with – I have not attempted to hide my own convictions. I will emphasise three of these here.

1. E. M. Forster's *Howards End* is subtitled *Only connect*. This is a good motto for Christians. I am convinced that faith, properly understood, connects with real life. Faith in God is for Monday as well as for Sunday. I am equally convinced that we don't need to re-write the ancient creeds to make this happen. My own faith is traditional and orthodox. I would urge that it is up-to-date, relevant and radical *because* of this.

> 2. Different issues and emphases surface at different times, and we must find appropriate ways of communicating our faith to our generation. But the truths themselves do not change. God's truth is still to be found in the Bible. God's love is still to be seen in Jesus. God's joy and power are still to be experienced in the Church. Such, at least, are my convictions, and they are set out in this book.

3. The Creed presents a set of beliefs which Christians hold in common. But this does not mean that the Church

should have hard edges. Let enquirers mix with believers. Let members voice their doubts, hesitations and worries. There are such things as honest doubt and honest enquiry. And there is such a thing as sitting on the fence . . .

HOW TO GET THE MOST OUT OF THIS BOOK

As a *study course* it can be used in various ways:

1. As an *eight-week study course*.
2. As a *Lent study course* (chapters 1–5) and *an Advent study course* (chapters 6–8).
3. As *two four-week courses* (1–4; pause; then 5–8).
4. As a Confirmation or Baptism Course.
5. As a *repeated study course*.
   Study groups often use a single sheet of notes. Because there is more (much more!) here, some groups might wish to repeat the eight-week course after an interval (a few months say, or perhaps a year). I suspect that there are enough questions here to keep the keenest group hard at it throughout the decade!

The course is designed to be flexible for the *individual reader* as well as for the group. It can be read:

(a) As an *ordinary book* – from cover to cover. If you use it like this, I hope you will include the *Questions* so that you can debate with yourself. For raising questions is a good way of making points, as *Prime Minister's Question Time* illustrates.
(b) As a *very short book*, e.g. by just reading *Getting Started, Setting It Out, Questions* and a few *Viewpoints*.

A WORD ABOUT GROUPS

Please . . .

1. *Do not attempt to cover all the questions.* What matters is lively discussion, not completing the course. Red herrings and tangents are often productive – provided the herring isn't transformed into a hobbyhorse.
2. *Do play your part.* The quality of discussion does not depend upon the leader but upon the members. Examine yourself. If you know you talk too much, ration your contributions. If you never say anything, why not decide that every week you will speak at least twice (or once if you are *very* timid!)?

Groups thrive when members are prepared to become vulnerable. One main intention of discussion groups is to get to know what makes other people tick. So I hope that every member will be prepared to make himself/herself vulnerable by sharing doubts, fears, joys – and by articulating half-formed ideas.

A WORD ABOUT BOOKS

In order to give a wide spread of viewpoints I have quoted freely from other authors. I am grateful to all who toil with the pen, for I have learned a great deal from the printed page.

The word 'toil' perhaps betrays too much. Over the years I have produced several books/booklets (see page 2). Most of the material in *Know Your Faith* is new, but where I have already written on a topic in a way which seems relevant to this purpose, I have freely 'borrowed' from an earlier book.

I should like to know how groups have got on with this course – a line to me c/o Hodder and Stoughton will be forwarded. If your discussion goes well, you might care to know that *The Case Against Christ* (Hodder 1986), may be issued with a *Study Guide* for group discussion.

* * *

'I believe we live in critical days for the Christian faith. The forces of materialism and apathy militate against a strong and vigorous faith. Yet, curiously, the rise of secularism coincides with a growing paganism, interest in spiritualism, New Age religions and other forms of faith. There is only one response possible: Christians must know their faith and present it positively. I am delighted to commend John Young's book warmly. He is very well known for his previous writings on Christian basics and *Know Your Faith* will be a major resource for parish groups and individuals.'

The Most Rev Dr George Carey,
Archbishop of Canterbury

'John Young has a great gift for communicating profound ideas simply and readably. His skills were never more needed as the Churches launch into the Decade of Evangelism. I hope many will learn to know their Faith better by sharing in this discussion of it, and learning from an experienced guide.'

The Most Rev Dr John Habgood,
Archbishop of York

I Believe

'Therefore, since we have been justified through faith, we have peace with God through our Lord Jesus Christ' (Rom. 5:1).

'Immediately the boy's father exclaimed, "I do believe; help me overcome my unbelief!"' (Mark 9:24).

GETTING STARTED

Jackie Pullinger has developed a remarkable ministry among drug addicts in the Walled City of Hong Kong. Her achievements are so striking that her work has been widely reported, especially on television. In *Chasing the Dragon* Jackie explains how she ended up in Hong Kong.

Shortly after her conversion to Christ, she heard God speaking to her. 'Go, trust me, and I will lead you,' said a quiet voice. So she gave up teaching music, went to help a London vicar and waited for the next move. But nothing happened – so she explained her dilemma to the vicar:

I told him God and I had reached a stalemate; He told me clearly to go – and I knew why I was to go, but He would not tell me where. So how could I go?

Richard's reply was extraordinary. 'If God is telling you to go – you had better go.'

'How can I – I don't know where to. All my applications have been rejected.'

'Well, if you've tried all the conventional ways and

missionary societies, and God still is telling you to go, you had better get on the move.'

I felt frustrated.

'If you had a job, a ticket, accommodation, a sick fund and a pension, you wouldn't need to trust Him,' Richard continued. 'Anyone can go that way whether they are Christians or not. If I were you I would go out and buy a ticket for a boat going on the longest journey you can find and pray to know where to get off.'

I did not exactly hear bells but this was the first time in all those months of searching that anything made sense.

'It sounds terrific – but it must be cheating because I'd love to do that.' I still had the idea that anything to do with God had to be serious. I was sure that Christians always had to take the hard way and enjoyment was no part of suffering for their faith.

But Richard Thompson told me that it was quite scriptural. Abraham was willing to leave his country and follow Jehovah to a promised land without knowing where he was going because he trusted. In the same way thousands of years later Gladys Aylward journeyed in faith to China.

'You can't lose if you put yourself completely in God's hands, you know.' Richard was quite serious, 'If he doesn't want you to get on the ship he is quite able to stop you – or to make the ship go anywhere in the world . . . Maybe you will go all the way round the world just to talk to one sailor about Christ, or maybe you will go as far as Singapore and play the piano for a week of youth meetings and then come back.'

Richard's advice was extraordinary, but completely wise . . . I had simply to follow wherever God led. I, too, felt I could not lose on this adventure.

So I went out and after counting up my money found the cheapest ship on the longest route passing through the most countries on its way. It was from France to Japan – I bought a ticket and was all set.

(Extract from *Chasing the Dragon* [Hodder 1980]. Jackie's remarkable story is continued in *Crack in the Wall* [Hodder 1989].)

SETTING IT OUT

FAITH IS . . . Unavoidable
. . . Personal
. . . Scientific

1. FAITH IS . . . UNAVOIDABLE. 'I *believe* in the right of a woman to have an abortion,' says one person. 'I *believe* the unborn child has rights too,' argues another. 'I *believe* we should get rid of nuclear weapons,' asserts someone else. 'I *believe* those weapons have kept the peace for forty years,' claims his opponent. *I believe* . . . in the birch for hooligans; in capital punishment for terrorists; in experimentation on embryos; in Marxism; in capitalism; in freedom of speech; in censorship . . .

If challenged, people who make such statements attempt to produce arguments. They give reasons to support their beliefs – their commitment to a cause, an ideal, a way of life. Emotions run high, but facts and arguments are important as well. These make various beliefs seem reasonable to those who hold them – even though they know that other viewpoints claim to be based on evidence too.

Our beliefs undergird the way we think and behave; they make us the sort of people we are. Most causes that *really* matter to us have words like 'faith' or 'belief' attached to them. Believing is a crucial – and universal – activity. Faith is not just for religious people; it is an inescapable fact of life for everyone.

Recently I've heard influential people assert that faith and trust are central to the following vital areas of life; international politics; economic affairs; the relationship between doctor and patient. (And tennis at Wimbledon!)

We all live by probability and there is no opting out of belief. Faith is not a question of believing one hundred impossible things before breakfast. Christians are called 'believers', but we all base our lives on assumptions which cannot be proved with mathematical certainty.

Christians *believe* that God exists. Atheists *believe* that God does not exist. Agnostics *believe* that we don't have enough evidence to decide. The indifferent person *believes* that it doesn't matter either way.

A vicar visited a home to arrange a funeral. The dead man was 'big' in horse racing. 'Are you a betting-man, Vicar?' asked his son. 'You bet I am,' said the Vicar, to that man's surprise. He went on to explain that every single day he bet his life on the promises of God.

It is not a question of *whether* we believe but *what* we believe – and whether our beliefs are backed up by the available evidence. For not all acts of faith are equally likely to be true, as bookies will tell you.

2. FAITH IS . . . PERSONAL. *A Parable*. My friend was accused of stealing from a supermarket. He was caught outside the shop with groceries for which he had not paid. He protested his innocence and I *believed* him.

> When St Paul said, 'The life I now live I live by faith in the Son of God who loved me and gave Himself for me,' he was not setting himself apart from the world by virtue of his faith, but only by virtue of Him in whom he put his faith . . . The world is divided therefore not between those who believe and those who do not believe, but between those who believe in the powers of the world and those who believe in the Power of God. (Lord Blanch, Archbishop of York: 1975–1983.)

Perhaps I was being sentimental and allowing friendship to overrule clear thinking. Or perhaps I was being stupid – refusing to face facts. But I don't think so. I accepted the evidence against him and so did he, for he did not deny possessing the goods. The point is, there were other relevant *facts* which kept my *faith* in my friend alive.

I knew he was very honest: only the week before he had handed in a bulging wallet to the local police. I knew too that he was forgetful – and that he was under stress. So I believed him when he explained that he put the goods into his own bag rather than the supermarket basket, because his mind was not on his shopping trip.

As it happens, the Court agreed with me. The *facts* made my *faith* in my friend both reasonable and right. So he was declared innocent and allowed to go free.

3. FAITH IS . . . SCIENTIFIC. When I started reading books on the philosophy of science I was surprised to discover the importance of faith in science itself. A belief that the laws of nature will remain constant is at the foundation of the scientific quest. No one can prove (in the strict sense

of that word) that nature will behave in the future as it has in the past; or that the same laws apply throughout the universe. But unless they *believe* these things to be true, scientists cannot get to work.

When trying to decide between two rival explanations, scientists usually opt for the simpler, more 'graceful' explanation. They *believe* this to be a sound guide to the way the world is.

Of course, these beliefs are extremely reasonable. But they are *beliefs*. These viewpoints cannot be proved conclusively, but without such acts of faith we cannot make sense of our world.

PROBING THE MEANING

What follows? LOTS! For example . . .

> FAITH . . . governs action
> . . . is twinned with facts
> . . . needs care and attention
> . . . needs secure foundations
> . . . is linked with real life
> . . . does not banish anguish
> . . . can cope with doubt

1. FAITH . . . GOVERNS ACTION. 'It doesn't matter what you believe as long as you are sincere. It's what you *do* that matters, not what you believe.' People often say these things when they discuss religion. But beliefs and actions are tied together.

If you believe the gods are pleased by human sacrifice, then it's tough on your children. If your witch doctor believes that a hole bored in your head will cure headaches, it's tough on you. If the terrorist who hijacks your plane sincerely believes in his cause, you are in for a rough ride.

We are right to value sincerity, but false beliefs – even sincerely held false beliefs – can be disastrous. Indeed, the more sincere your 'doctor' is about boring a hole in your head, the worse it will be. And the really sincere terrorist is the most dangerous of all.

Belief governs action.

2. FAITH . . . IS TWINNED WITH FACTS. This is sometimes disputed. For example, the great atheist philosopher Bertrand Russell argued like this: 'We may define faith as a firm belief in something for which there is no evidence. Where there is evidence, no one speaks of faith. We do not speak of faith that two and two make four, or that the world is round. We only speak of faith when we wish to substitute emotion for evidence.'

There is an important error here. 'Where there is evidence, no one speaks of faith,' asserts Bertrand Russell. But we *do*. Despite the supermarket incident, I continue to believe in the honesty of my friend *for various good reasons*. My *faith* is based on *evidence* – the fact of his good track record, for example. Bertrand Russell himself believed in a great many causes. Did he never say, 'I believe in *this* cause for *these* reasons'?

3. FAITH . . . NEEDS CARE AND ATTENTION. 'He lost his faith.' We sympathise as though it is unavoidable – like losing a loved one. But some losses are avoidable: we can lose things through carelessness or indifference.

In our secular and superstitious world, *un*belief in the living God is in the air we breathe. So we need to be

vigilant, alert and thoughtful, or we may simply drift
away from the Christian faith. Not because we come
across convincing new reasons for not believing – but
because it's easier to follow the crowd. Jesus made this
clear in his famous Parable of the Sower (Matthew 13:3–
9). Perhaps 2 Timothy 4:10 is the saddest verse in the
whole Bible? Hebrews 2.1 is certainly one of the clearest.

> If we wish to be rational, not now and then but
> constantly, we must pray for the gift of faith, for the
> power to go on believing, not in the teeth of reason,
> but in the teeth of lust, and terror, and jealousy, and
> boredom, and indifference. (C. S. Lewis.)

4. FAITH . . . NEEDS SECURE FOUNDATIONS. For many
people, faith in God starts with intuition. They look at the
stars, or a sunset, or a tiny baby and they say, 'There
simply *must* be a Mind behind it all.' This is fine as far
as it goes. But intuitive faith like that can easily be
shaken. Strong Christian faith is based on *evidence* and
on *experience*.

If asked why I believe in God, I will point in two
directions. *First, away from myself* and towards Jesus of
Nazareth. It is extremely difficult to make sense of Jesus –
his life, his claims, his character, his teaching – without
using Christian terms such as Son of God, the Light and
Saviour of the World. *Second, I look into myself.* When I
do this, I find the Spirit of Jesus living within me. This is a
mixed blessing! He is the *Holy* Spirit. In addition to
encouragement and comfort, he brings tough challenges.

He brings assurance too (Ephesians 1:13–14). I am
sure that Jesus is alive and that he accompanies me
through life. This unshakeable conviction arises from

promises in the Bible and from deep personal experience over many years. It is shared by countless other believers. These factors do not exclude doubt; but doubt does not overwhelm and engulf us. We hold on to God. More to the point . . . he holds on to us.

5. FAITH . . . IS LINKED WITH REAL LIFE. We worship a Monday God not just a Sunday God. Faith is not reserved for a special area of life labelled 'religion'; it is for everyday use. Jesus encouraged his hearers to trust God. In his own life he showed us faith in action, and in his teaching he spelt out what faith involves. In the Sermon on the Mount (Matthew 5–7), Jesus made it clear that faith is essentially *practical* and essentially *simple*.

Think of God as a very good father and you will understand what faith means. Good parents are interested in the major events in the lives of their children: their schooling, career, marriage. But they are also interested in the small details of daily living: their games, their cuts and bruises, their joys and disappointments.

Think of God like that, said Jesus. Let your trust and dependence be like that of a little child. Let peace replace anxiety; let worry give way to joy. In all you do, take God's love and power into account.

Now teaching like that is easy and hard at the same time. It is certainly uncomplicated, and simple people can sometimes grasp it more readily than the sophisticated and clever (Matthew 11:25). But it is hard in the *practical* sense. Like jumping from a high diving-board, it is straight-forward but (for most of us) rather difficult in practice.

Especially when things get really tough.

6. FAITH . . . DOES NOT BANISH ANGUISH. Recently I conducted a very painful funeral service. Two tiny coffins and one distraught family.

We live in a beautiful and exciting world. But it is an unpredictable, dangerous and frightening world too. God has created our world with a 'life of its own'. Accidents *happen*; they are not 'sent'. Jesus made this clear. The sun (which gives life, but can destroy) shines on the righteous and the unrighteous (Matthew 5:45). Towers fall on innocent people (Luke 13:4). When bad things happen to good people, we are forced to ask deep questions. Questions like: do we *really* find love, purpose and God at the heart of the universe – or do we live in a madhouse ruled by empty nothingness?

Faith does not mean that we must pretend. We feel anguish, pain and uncertainty, and we don't have answers to all our deep questions. The Christian Faith is coherent but it isn't always neat and tidy. Christianity is not 'a filleted religion' – it comes to us with loose ends and bones. It does not trade in slick answers; it does ring true to real life. 'I don't know the answer' is a quite proper Christian response to some questions.

What we *can* say is this. We know that God loves us because of two wonderful gifts – the gift of his Son and the gift of his Spirit. Jesus lived for us, died for us and lives within us. So we can feel confident. Whatever life throws at us, we know that in the long term 'all shall be well, and all shall be well, and all manner of thing shall be well' (Mother Julian of Norwich).

'. . . neither death nor life, neither angels nor demons, neither the present nor the future, nor any powers, neither height nor depth, nor anything else in all creation, will be able to separate us from the love of God that is in Christ Jesus our Lord' (Rom. 8:38–39).

> Being a Christian does not protect us from the difficulties involved in being a human being. Jesus nowhere promises that he will shield us from disappointment, or problems, or depression, or suffering. What he does promise is that he will be with us – giving strength and helping us to find meaning.

7. FAITH . . . CAN COPE WITH DOUBT. Jesus chided his disciples for their lack of faith (Matthew 14:31; Luke 9:40–41). But he did it gently and with understanding. In asking Peter to walk on water, and expecting Thomas to believe that he who had died was now alive, he was asking a great deal. And he knew it. So he rescued Peter despite his lack of faith; and he persisted with Thomas despite his stubbornness. This is an enormous encouragement to those modern Christians who often experience doubt.

But doubt is sometimes given too much significance in the modern Church. 'I've always had doubts. There's no real faith without doubts,' asserts Archbishop John Habgood. *But there is.* Some Christians have a doubt-free faith – an unshakeable sense of the presence of God. Rather inconsistently, the Archbishop recognised this when he said of one of his illustrious predecessors, 'William Temple saw it as a weakness in himself that he had had no real experience of doubt, because it made it difficult for him to stand alongside those for whom the life of faith made no sense.'

Of course it is important to be honest about our doubts. Pretence has no place in the Christian life. But perhaps the crucial thing is not how we *feel* but how we *behave*. Daily obedience is required of all Christians – whether we are feeling full of faith or full of doubt at that particular time. Christian faith is inescapably linked with Christian commitment.

The letter to the Hebrews makes this clear. The great honour roll-call (Hebrews 11) is about *faith in action*. Faith has a passive side. 'Relax! God loves you.' We are encouraged to 'let go and let God'. But faith which simply makes us *feel* good without *doing* good is not true faith. 'The only thing that counts is faith expressing itself through love' (Gal. 5:6).

CORE QUESTIONS . . .

For Group Discussion and Individual Reflection

1. (a) Take a few moments to tick the following grid. Then pool your convictions on *one* of these issues.

CAUSE	Strongly in favour	Strongly against	Not sure	It depends
Abortion				
Nuclear weapons				
Birch for hooligans				
Capital punishment for terrorists				

Censorship				
Embryo experimentation				
Smacking children				
Choose your own!				

    (b) As you discuss *one* issue, are facts and arguments used – or is it just a matter of intuition?

2. Four Questions about faith, doubt – and Archbishops!
The Archbishop of York said, 'I've always had doubts. There's no real faith without doubts.' Yet Archbishop William Temple had few doubts.

    (a) Which of these links more closely with *your* experience?

    (b) Do you agree with the Archbishop of York that 'there's no real faith without doubts'?

    (c) Archbishop William Temple felt that experience of doubt by Christians is necessary for effective evangelism in a doubting world. Do you agree?

    (d) Archbishop George Carey claims that 'doubt has stirred me to deeper faith'. Can you relate to that?

3. In the remarkable example of faith at the beginning, Jackie Pullinger went on a 'crazy' journey. *Partly* as a result of an inner conviction that God had spoken to her. *Partly* because Richard (her vicar) encouraged her. She said, 'Richard's advice was extraordinary, but completely wise.'

(a) Was it? Would you give that sort of 'risky' anti-commonsense advice?

(b) Do you look for guidance from God when making decisions? If so, how?

4. An enquirer asks you to give one concrete example of your own faith in action (responding to illness, coping with a problem, taking on a task, or . . .). What would you say? A few minutes to allow jottings on paper might help this one go with a swing.

5. Some Christians argue that insurance policies and faith in God don't mix. Peace of mind should come, *not* from the security of cash but from trust in God. He will protect us from, or see us through, accidents and disaster. Do you agree with this?

BIBLE STUDY. All Christians have faith – by definition. And all would agree that faith is a gift from God. But when St Paul lists different gifts to be found within the Church, he includes faith as a special gift possessed by some but not by others. (See 1 Corinthians 12:7–9 and Romans 12:6.) How do you make sense of that?

. . . AND MORE QUESTIONS

Why more questions? First, to help groups which meet regularly; you may have discussed the topics covered by CORE QUESTIONS recently. Second, because posing questions is a good way of emphasising points. If you doubt this – watch Prime Minister's Question Time! Third, because this study course contains more material than most. So some groups will wish to tackle it twice (the second time after an interval of several months or a year). Groups which do this will wish to use different questions.

*Perhaps I should add that I hope individuals will read
all the questions – but that groups will not tackle them all.
What matters is lively, honest discussion at a leisurely
pace. If a single question generates that – FINE!*

6. In the ASB Baptism/Confirmation Services we say, 'I
   believe and trust' in God. What, if anything, do the
   words 'and trust' add to the phrase 'I believe'?

7. Accidents *happen*; they are not *sent* (Page 28). Do
   you agree? (See Matt. 5:45 and 10:29–31; Luke
   13:4,5; Rom. 8:28 and Heb. 12:7.)

8. Some versions of the Nicene Creed begin, 'We
   believe . . .' The Apostles' Creed – which started life
   as a confession or testimony for baptismal candidates – requires us to say, 'I believe . . .' Do you
   prefer 'I' or 'We'?

9. A Buddhist once asked me, 'How do you think about
   God?' i.e. how do you visualise him? As a person; as
   a 'thing'; as a colour . . . ? He went on to ask what
   my mind focused on in prayer. What would you say?

10. (a) Pick out one passage which strikes you as es-
        pecially interesting, important, infuriating or
        difficult. Why? (You might prefer to read *View-
        points* first).
    (b) Do you agree with my 3 'convictions' on page
        15?

11. Consider these phrases: *bad faith, blind faith, leap of
    faith, loss of faith, halfway to faith.*

12. (a) What, if anything, makes you unsure/sure con-
        cerning your own faith in God?

(b) What would you most like clarified concerning the Christian faith?

13. 'A load of old-fashioned superstition.' How would you defend your faith in God against this charge?

14. 'Christian faith is inescapably linked with Christian commitment' (Page 30). How does this work:
    (a) in your use of time, talents and money?
    (b) in your relationships?

15. 'My faith is a very private matter.' Is that a valid statement for a Christian?

16. Some Christians grow up in the faith – like Timothy. Others are catapulted into faith in Jesus – like Paul. Share stories of how you came to faith. (Remember that some people may be halfway to faith or without faith. No pressure please!).

VIEWPOINTS

SOME DEFINITIONS:

· Faith is being 90 per cent sure 90 per cent of the time but 100 per cent committed.

· Faith is wishful thinking.

· Faith is behaving as though something were certain when the evidence only makes it probable.

· Faith is unconsidered opinion.

· Faith is superstition made respectable.

· Faith involves living with questions that we cannot answer – in the light of the answers that we *do* have.

- 'Now Faith is being sure of what we hope for and certain of what we do not see' (Heb. 11.1).

- GERALD PRIESTLAND I hope I believe, I know that I trust.

- BISHOP DAVID JENKINS Simple faith is what keeps us all going.

- PAUL TILLICH To argue that God exists is to deny him.

- JOHN LOCKE He that believes without having any reason for believing may be in love with his own fancies.

- C. S. LEWIS Believe in God and you will have to face hours when it seems obvious that this material world is the only reality: disbelieve in God and you will have to face hours when this material world seems to shout at you that it is not all. No conviction, religious or irreligious, will of itself end once and for all this fifth-columnist in the soul. Only the practice of Faith resulting in the habit of Faith will gradually do that.

- JOHN VINCENT Our word *believe* does not get the force of the Greek word. It really means 'give yourself over to', 'risk your life on' . . . So Jesus says, don't hold yourself back. You will not get anything that way. Rather, let yourself go, 'get with it', take a chance, act as if it were true. The 'good news' is that the Kingdom is here. Let yourself start acting as if it is true.

- PHILIP CROWE The Bible does not contrast faith and knowledge nor does it imply that faith is a leap in the dark. The biblical contrast is between faith and sight. 'Faith is the evidence of things not seen.' 'We walk by faith, not by sight.' Far from contrasting faith and knowledge, in the New Testament to know God and to have faith in him are two ways of saying almost the same thing.

· **WILLIAM CAREY**   Expect great things from God; attempt great things for God.

· **IGNATIUS OF ANTIOCH**   c.35–c.107 The Christian life begins and ends with two qualities: faith, which is the beginning, and love which is the goal . . . The fruit of faith should be evident in our lives, for being a Christian is more than a matter of making sound professions of faith. It should reveal itself in practical and visible ways.

· **PROVOST DAVID L. EDWARDS**   There is no *proof* that God is real – if by 'proof' we mean the way it can be proved that this book exists or that $2+2=4$. God (if real) is just too big to be fitted into that kind of proof . . .

There is a kind of proof which you can have when thinking about God – and a kind of knowledge, too. It is the knowledge that you have when you say you 'believe' in a friend. It is the proof that you have when you love someone else and find yourself loved back . . . Your relationship with God can become like that. You still will not have complete certainty, but you will have enough confidence to decide that for all practical purposes you are prepared to bet your life that God is there . . .

There are many things . . . that make it hard to believe in God. Face up to them – otherwise you will be told that your faith isn't honest, and you may agree with your critics. There is darkness around us. But also light! For many things . . . are indeed hard to explain if there is no God and therefore no good purpose running through it all. Atheism has its problems.

· **ARCHBISHOP ROBIN EAMES** God is a very personal dimension in my own life. I believe that the evidence of His existence must be felt rather than proved. I believe He chose to show us His real nature through the life of His son, Jesus Christ . . . Of course I have my moments of doubt and uncertainty – and I have questions I cannot easily answer . . . But in the end I see so much evidence of the power of His love at work in the world in the lives of people I meet and work with, that I know in my own heart and mind He must be at the centre of what I call human experience.

· **DAVID BOND** Faith means living with the pressures of life, but letting Jesus take the stresses of life.

· **REINHARD BONNKE** Faith is eyesight; Jesus is the Light . . . Faith is an outstretched hand.

· **ANON** If the reality of God were small enough to be grasped, he would not be great enough to be adored.

· **C. S. LEWIS** Christianity is a statement which, if false, is of *no* importance, and, if true, of infinite importance. The one thing it cannot be is moderately important.

MEDITATION AND PRAYER

Just as there can be no actual swimming until you take the plunge, there can be no actual believing in God until we are prepared to follow Christ. (Archbishop George Carey).

I think the hand of God can be seen everywhere. (Professor Arnold Wolfendale: Astronomer Royal since 1991).

Read Hebrews 11:1–12. How sure do you have to be before you are prepared to trust and act? Think of examples such as standing surety or getting married.

Sit quietly and read the following prayer silently. Think of individuals who are covered by these topics – and mention their names out loud when the leader says the prayer.

Lord of faith and doubt, help us to love you when life is good and to trust you when life is tough.

Lord of light and darkness, give light to those who have lost their faith and banish darkness from those who have never known your love.

Lord of life and death, give hope to those who are bereaved, comfort those who are dying and strengthen those who care and serve.

Especially we remember before you . . .

We pray in the name of Jesus who is our Lord and Saviour, our Brother and our Friend. Amen.

Homework?

Read the story of the boy with epilepsy in Mark 9:14–32. Imagine yourself as the boy's father and consider his feelings when he said to Jesus, 'I do believe; help me overcome my unbelief.' Repeat the phrase slowly and apply it to your own problems, anxieties and hopes.

I Believe in God the Father Almighty

'Abba, Father' he said, 'everything is possible for you. Take this cup from me. Yet not what I will, but what you will' (Mark 14.36).

Praise be to the God and Father of our Lord Jesus Christ, the Father of compassion and the God of all comfort (2 Cor. 1.3).

GETTING STARTED

26th June (1935)   Calverton House
                                                Stony Stratford
                                                Bucks

Dear God,
If you feel lonely up in the sky would you like to come down and stay with us, you could sleep in the spier-room [sic] and you could bathe with us, and I think you would enjoy yourself.
Love from John

The letter, written by eight-year-old John Habgood, was put in an envelope, correctly stamped and posted and addressed to 'Our Father which art in Heaven'. The local postmaster, presumably not the intended recipient, opened it and returned the envelope and contents to John Habgood's father. The envelope was marked 'Return to sender'; thus there were no theological implications as would have arisen had the envelope

been marked 'Gone away' or 'Unknown at this address'.
(From *Living with Paradox*, the biography of Archbishop John Habgood; John Peart-Binns [DLT: 1987].)

* * *

A modern Jew retells a famous Bible story:

Now, you would think that God would pick someone young to start a new kind of people. Someone who hadn't seen much; who was perhaps mystic, deeply religious; who lived remote from worldly things. Well, God chose a middle-aged man who'd lived in large cities all his life. A mature man with a good-looking wife, no children, and well used to the good things. He had a good business, a fine home and many servants. His name was Abraham. Into whose mind God spoke of fantastic things, and who listened with perfect faith. Abraham, who did not question; and when God said up and go he upped and went . . .

Abraham was born in the City of Ur near the Persian Gulf where the River Euphrates empties. After he was married he moved with his wife, his father and his nephew, whom he was bringing up, to another city far north called Haran. Both Ur and Haran were civilized and sophisticated places . . . These cities had many temples. Well, the people had many gods. Gods of all shapes and sizes. Gods they could see and touch. Familiar gods. No home was complete without three or four. Regularly dusted.

So you can imagine what Abraham's family said when he told them that the GOD that spoke to him was a voice only: No idol; no *thing*; just a voice. They thought he was mad.

'Tell me again, my son,' said old Terah, his father, 'you say a god spoke to you. Which god? Which one?'

'The only one,' said Abraham. 'Don't ask me how I know he is the only real one. I can't tell you, I just know. All the other gods *we* made. This one made *us* – and everything else too . . .

The young man Lot has listened to everything without speaking . . .

'Well, son,' said Abraham, 'what about you? Grandfather won't be coming. I'm giving him the river house and four servants. Everything else we are taking with us. I need a second-in-command who knows my ways. What do you say?'

Lot grinned, 'I say, Yes please,' he said.

(From *Bible Stories*; David Kossoff [Collins 1968].)

* * *

No words, however pure or sacred, will fully describe God. Indian spiritual teachers say something about God to which we ought to listen. They say: 'Not that! Not that!' The same emphasis on the mystery of God is found in the Bible. For God can never be pinned down like a dead butterfly, reduced to a formula or reproduced in a photograph . . . Like shots which always miss their target, human words will always fall short of the glory of God. But the words can show in what direction the glory lies; however imperfectly, they can point to the reality . . .

(From *What Anglicans Believe*; David L. Edwards [Mowbray: Revised 1984].)

SETTING IT OUT

Images galore

The Old Testament is clear: the people of God must make no graven images. They obeyed (well, *some* of the time) and poured their considerable creative energies into architecture and words. Especially words . . . and those words painted pictures on the imagination.

Some years ago I led a Bible study on the Book of Psalms with a group of young people. We went on an 'image hunt' – looking for words which describe God. We gathered over thirty: Rock; Shield; Fortress; King; Shepherd; Judge; Father . . .

Jesus was soaked in the Psalms and he emphasised three of these pictures. (You might work at the question 'Which three?' See Page 56 for my suggestions.) One of these was *Father*. Indeed, he prayed to God as *Abba* Father – using an Aramaic children's word for 'Daddy'.

Jesus clearly felt that this domestic word reflects God's love, care and concern in every detail of our lives. For good parents are concerned not only with the 'big' events in their children's lives. They are concerned with their visits to the park, with their fear of the dark, with . . .

The apostle Peter, who often heard Jesus talk of the heavenly Father who counts every hair on our heads, could write: 'Cast all your anxiety on him because he cares for you' (1 Pet. 5.7). The old saying is true: if a thing is big enough to *worry* about, it is big enough to *pray* about. The God to whom Jesus points is not a philosophical 'First Cause'. He is the God of love who is to be trusted in daily life.

Of course, this position is not without its problems, and we turn to these now.

PROBING THE MEANING

Seven issues

The teaching of Jesus gives enormous encouragement and strength to countless believers. God is our heavenly Father who can be trusted day-in, day-out. But this same description also raises questions.

1. *Almighty and loving God?* A few years ago I came across a book called *God Almighty and Ills Unlimited*. This title highlights the old conundrum. If God is *Almighty*, and if God is *Love*: why suffering? – especially accidents? For it looks as though God does not have enough power to stop them (in which case he is not almighty) *or* that he does not care enough to bother (in which case, he is not love).

2. *Father God?* Many children have a loving relationship with their fathers – so the phrase Heavenly Father conveys a positive picture of God. Can that term be rescued for a child who associates the word *father* with anger, or fear, or abuse? And what about single-parent families where the father does not play his traditional role?

3. *Mother God?* Some people claim that referring to God as Father is an example of male imperialism. If we want to speak of God's love, why not *Motherly* care? (as in Isaiah 66:12–13).

4. *Personal God?* Others feel that God has more than enough to do, running a complex universe. In their

view, prayer for ourselves and our loved ones is arrogant. How can we matter to God personally and individually? ('He simply *can't* be bothered with little me . . .')

5. *Creator God?* The Apostles' Creed goes on, '*I believe in God, the Father almighty, creator of heaven and earth.*'
   (a) What do we mean by calling God 'Creator'? How does teaching about creation in the Bible square with modern scientific theories like 'the big bang' or evolution? This continues to be a real stumbling block. A recent survey showed that many teenagers continue to believe that science disproves religion. While reading that report I spoke with a university scientist who told me that several of his colleagues are Christians. It seems that many *real* scientists have few problems with the 'science and religion' issue – yet the popular, damaging view persists. How can we get the truth across?
   (b) The Bible says that God has given us the stewardship of our world. What does this mean for our attitude to Green issues?

6. *Jealous God?* Like it or not, belief in God the Father *excludes* some other beliefs. This is clear from the Old Testament: belief in the LORD meant rejection of the fertility gods who demanded ritual prostitution and child sacrifice. In some ways we are light years from this problem; but in other ways it is very modern. Astrology for example. We are naturally curious – often anxious – about the future. The Bible encourages us to face the unknown with trust and confidence in the living God, and this rules out horoscopes and

fortune-tellers. (There will be an opportunity to discuss this later.)

7. *Saving God?* If God is holy and we are sinful, how can we be saved? The Bible appears to speak with two voices. St Paul insists that salvation is by God's grace, through faith. St James seems to say that we are justified by what we *do*. How can this contrast be resolved? (See page 56 for my suggested solution to this puzzle.)

The problem of pain

At this point we shall concentrate on the first difficulty — the question of suffering. In fact, this raises two problems. The first is practical: how can we *cope* with it? The second is theoretical: how can we *understand* it? This second question is set out by psychologist Dr H. J. Eysenck, who states the atheist objection with great clarity:

> . . . as a scientist, I require proof for any assertion, and no such proof for the existence of God has been forthcoming. In the second place, there is a logical inconsistency between a belief in an all-powerful, all-merciful God and the existence of evil in the world.

Professor Eysenck raises a big question for all who believe in God. But his argument is not as watertight as he likes to think. This is suggested by the fact that some other psychologists and philosophers continue to believe in God — even though they are well aware of this line of reasoning.

Dr Eysenck says that he requires proof for any assertion. But atheism involves an act of faith too. 'I believe
that the universe and life came into existence without
God' claims the atheist. It is quite impossible for him to
prove this.

His assertion – like the Christian counterclaim – is a
statement of faith. And we could argue that the burden of
proof is on *him* – given the fact that most people make
sense of the world by believing in some sort of God. (See
Professor Swinburne's *Viewpoint* on Page 55.)

Atheists often base their beliefs upon the existence of
suffering and evil. And I readily concede that these
produce huge problems for those of us who believe in a
loving God. There are no easy answers, but this does
not mean that we can say nothing. In response to this
challenge we shall consider a modern parable, and a
devastating event:

(a) *A son is killed* During the Gulf war Mr Brown was
involved with the Kuwaiti Resistance movement. He
was introduced to Dr Rajab who, he was told, was
head of the whole operation. They worked together
and Brown was tremendously impressed with Rajab.

On one occasion they planned to blow up an
ammunition store. It was almost certain that those who
took part would die. Rajab's son volunteered and with
much grief Rajab allowed him to go. The mission was
successful but his son was killed.

One day Rajab told Brown that they must alter their
tactics. He warned Brown that he would see him doing
things which he would not understand. On occasions,

Brown saw Rajab helping their own men to escape. At other times Brown saw him standing by while their men were handed over to the Iraqis. Sometimes Rajab even appeared in the uniform of the enemy. 'He is a traitor!' cried Brown's comrades.

But Brown knew Rajab. In particular, he knew that he had allowed his son to die for the cause. Because of this, Brown was convinced that Rajab could be trusted. He was often bewildered, but he was sure that there must be a reason, and that everything would make sense in the end.

The atheist is in the position of Brown's comrades. He considers only part of the evidence – the fact of suffering.

The Christian is like Brown. He is often bewildered by occurrences which he cannot understand. His faith is sorely tried by terrible events which suggest that God does not care – or that he does not exist. But he knows God. Above all he knows that God sent his Son to die for us. It is because of this that he continues to base his life on the belief that God loves him – despite some appearances to the contrary.

Let's move from a modern parable to a recent tragedy:

(b) *A father dies* It happened on a Saturday afternoon in autumn. The sun was shining, so Dad volunteered to take the children into the countryside while Mum stayed at home. He lay down on the grass and the children went to explore. Eventually they returned, for it was time to go home. Dad was still lying down so they went to wake him up. At least, they *tried* to wake him . . .

But they couldn't. And they didn't. For Dad was dead – leaving three very frightened children.

A few weeks later I visited their mother. As I drove to her home I wondered how I would be greeted. Would she blame God? Would she say, 'I'll never call God Father again'? (as someone else said, with understandable bitterness, following a terrible accident). Would she be stunned into silence?

. In fact she welcomed me – and said that through the whole ghastly episode, God had been very close and very real to her. Of course she didn't *understand*. To the question *why*? she could give no answer. But about the question '*Does God care*?' she was quite clear. And she continued to think of God as her loving Father.

> This is the authentic voice of faith. People with a living faith are often bewildered. But they are prepared to live with questions which they cannot answer, in the light of the great answers which they *do* possess.

Such faith is not a blind refusal to face facts. Rather, it comes from a concern to take *all* the facts into account. The fact of suffering: yes. But the fact of Christ too. *And* the fact of extra strength 'from somewhere'.

That woman's experience is not unusual. Suffering sometimes embitters. People lose their faith in God, or resent his apparent inactivity. When he heard that his wife had died, one man flattened a nurse (because medicine had failed her) and bent the metal cross in the Hospital Chapel (because God had failed her).

But many people testify to the God who has strengthened and softened them through their ordeal.

Wishful thinking can play a part of course. (I refuse to believe that my husband or child has ceased to exist – so I invent God and heaven.) But I doubt that this is true in every case. Such experiences of God often seem to be very real and remarkably sustaining – and sometimes life-changing too. They also seem to link firmly with the experience of thousands of other people – not all of whom are impressionable, muddled or escapist.

CORE QUESTIONS . . .

For Group Discussion and Individual Reflection
Take time to fill in questions 1, 2 and 3 on your own, before discussing your answers.

*Please asterisk. Use one * if the reason is important for you; none if it doesn't apply at all; lots if it is very, very important.*

1. I believe in God because:

   (a) of the beauty around me   ....
   (b) of harmony in nature   ....
   (c) I instinctively 'know' that he is there   ....
   (d) of a personal experience   ....
   (e) of a whole range of personal experiences   ....
   (f) of what I read in the Bible   ....
   (g) of Jesus Christ   ....
   (h) of people I have met   ....
   (i) of the Church   ....
   (j) ....

2. My faith in God is: True/False
   (a) never clouded with doubts   ....
   (b) sometimes clouded with doubts   ....
   (c) often clouded with doubts   ....
   (d) something which comes and   ....
       goes
   (e) a fairly recent thing   ....
   (f) something I have always had   ....
   (g) too personal to talk about   ....
   (h) something I want to share with   ....
       others
   (i) non-existent   ....
   (j) ....

3. (a) Do you think that some of your non-Christian
       friends believe in God 'deep-down'?   YES/NO
   (b) If 'yes', do you know/can you guess, why they
       stop short of Church membership and Christian
       discipleship?

If you are in a group, compare notes for 1, 2 and 3.

4. I overheard a conversation in church between two
   women. The younger woman had two problems —
   firstly with the maleness of God; secondly with the
   notion that she was a *Son* of God (Romans 8.14). The
   older woman thought she was making a lot of fuss
   about nothing.

   Where do *you* stand? Read Dorothy McMahon's
   Viewpoint on Page 56. She argues that these issues
   are vital, because they prevent many women from
   accepting the Gospel in a deep, personal way. Is she
   right — or is this a case of fashionable Christian
   feminism?

5. Do not be afraid, little flock . . . (Luke 12:32). Therefore do not worry about tomorrow (Matt. 6:34).

(a) Faith in God rules out horoscopes. Does it? Discuss *Jealous God?* on Page 44.

(b) List common superstitions. Are they compatible with faith in God?

BIBLE STUDY. Read Psalm 13 and Psalm 10:1; 16–18.

I talked recently to two mothers whose babies had died. Both were believers and both were full of grief – but their responses were very different. One felt anger; she thought she was losing her faith in God. The other felt that her faith had never been stronger.

(a) Share similar experiences – from your own life or from the lives of friends.

(b) Are anger and anguish valid forms of prayer? If so, should we use them more?

(c) . Do you know people who have been made bitter by suffering – or those who have come through suffering with hearts softened and faith strengthened?

. . . AND MORE QUESTIONS

(Please read the note on page 32 entitled *Why More Questions* at this point.

6. 'I believe in God, the Father Almighty. Christian prayer is based on this phrase from the Creed. If a new Christian asked you to teach him/her to pray, what would you say?

7. Do group members know people whose experience as children makes the word 'father' a 'bad' word? Is

this a barrier for them to faith in God? If so, what can
be done about it?

8. Most people (about 75 per cent) claim to believe in
   God, yet a bishop recently said that we live in a
   Godless society. In what sense is he right – if he is?

9. Because of Bible teaching about creation and
   stewardship, all Christians must be 'Green'. True or
   False – or partly true/partly false?

10. A friend is interested in, but uncertain about,
    Christianity.

    (a) She asks, 'Why do you believe in God? What
         exactly do you mean by "faith"?' What is your
         answer?
    (b) She presses on: 'What practical differences
         would faith in God make to my life?' What
         would you say? Illustrate your answer from life
         – yours or other people's.

11. Read these quotations:

    'God calls us all to this crazy adventure of being
    Christians . . . which is by far the highest wisdom'
    (Archbishop John Habgood).

    'We all have to choose between two ways of being
    crazy: the foolishness of the Gospel and the non-
    sense of the values of our world' (Jean Vanier).

    Ever since Abraham, faith in God has had its zany
    aspects.

    (a) Do you welcome this?
    (b) Do you fear this?
    (c) Can it go too far?

(d) How important is reason in your faith?

(e) How important are feelings in your faith?

12. Imagine that you have three problems: over a relationship; over health; over a difficult decision.

    (i) How would you tackle these? Would God come into it in any way? (Be honest!)

    (ii) Can you recall a real situation where you did 'involve' God?

    (iii) Does the question give an unduly negative slant; i.e. does it suggest that we can keep God in reserve to help with problems – a bit like a genie in a lamp. Do we? Do you? If so, what can we do about it?

13. Do you have views on issue 5(a) on Page 44?
BIBLE STUDY. Read Acts 7:54–8:2. We have been considering suffering and death. On the Christian view, death is the gateway to the glorious life of heaven. This was very clear to Stephen (Acts 7:56–59). Yet his friends mourned deeply (8:2).

(a) When someone close to us dies, is there a balance to be struck between joy and sorrow – or does it just 'happen'?

(b) Do you know people who feel guilt at the way they have reacted to bereavement? Can we help them? How?

VIEWPOINTS

· **BERNARD WEATHERILL** (When he was Speaker of the House of Commons, referring to his faith in God.) It's absolutely crucial to me.

· **PAUL BOATENG** (Labour MP) The hymn 'Blessed

Assurance' encapsulates one of the wonders of our faith – that is, a certainty that come what may, Christ will see you through.

- **JOHN BIFFEN** (Conservative MP, commenting on Psalm 121.) *I lift up my eyes to the hills – Where does my help come from? My help comes from the Lord, the maker of Heaven and earth:* I think I have learnt over the years that there is much merit and meaning in those words.

- **ARCHBISHOP GEORGE CAREY** The presence of a personal creator makes sense of our place in the scheme of things and unites the world of nature and humankind which atheism divides.

- **JONATHAN MILLER** Earthquakes I can put up with. Pillars of salt – fine. Inundations – perfectly reasonable. They're all dealt with in the clauses of insurance contracts. What I think is insufferable on the part of God – if in fact there is a God – is to have invented a creature who visits more suffering upon himself than inanimate nature can inflict. That, I think, is something for which God should be at Nuremberg.

- **DAVID JENKINS** (Bishop of Durham) God is wonderful and God wants us and because he is so wonderful and loving he waits for us . . . to respond to him.

- **PROFESSOR JOHN POLKINGHORNE** The Christian God is not a detached if compassionate beholder of the sufferings of the world, he is a participant in them. It is the crucified God whom we worship.

- **BISHOP RICHARD HARRIES** Suffering is contrary to the will of God. In the Gospels Jesus' ministry is an invasion of the forces of goodness and light against all that blights and hurts human life . . . a sharp distinction has to be made between what God directly wills and what he merely permits as part of his overall purpose. So a parent may be responsible for giving his child permission to drive the family car. But he in no sense wills the subsequent accident.

- **JOHN MORTIMER** I can't accept the idea of an omnipotent creator who allows the gassing of seven million Jews, or children dying of leukaemia, or the horrors that are going on in Cambodia and South America. I can't find his excuse for that . . . Christianity becomes a religion of suffering . . . in which people can be reconciled to their poverty and their ill-health and their lot in this world, without people having to bother to rectify it.

- **PROVOST DAVID L. EDWARDS** Why does anything exist, rather than nothing? If the universe is nothing more than an accident, how has it happened that it contains so much order and so much beauty? It has been said that it works like a machine, yet sleeps like a picture.

 Is the universe merely a lottery or a bingo hall? If so, how has it happened that there has been such amazing progress? How has sheer chance produced Shakespeare and Beethoven, Einstein and Rembrandt?

- **PROFESSOR RICHARD SWINBURNE** Why believe that there is a God at all? My answer is to suppose that there is a God explains why there is a world at all; why there are the scientific laws there are; why animals and then human beings have evolved; why humans have the opportunity to mould their characters and those of their fellow humans for good or ill and to change the environment in which we live; why we have the well-authenticated account of Christ's life, death and resurrection; why throughout the centuries men have had the apparent experience of being in touch with and guided by God; and so much else. In fact, the hypothesis of the existence of God makes sense of the whole of our experience better than any other explanation . . .

· **DOROTHY MCMAHON**   There is no doubt in my mind that women sit in the pews of the churches year after year and fail to hear the Gospel. They listen to the Word like observers – they appreciate it, but they never claim it as their own. I believe that sexist language – that which excludes women and offers them only a male image of God – is a salvation issue. To ignore it is to be careless and half-hearted about the communication of the Gospel.

Two 'answers'

Jesus taught us to think of God as Father, Shepherd and King. He is to be trusted, loved, obeyed and feared. (See Page 42)

On Page 45 we looked at the apparent clash between St Paul and St James. One insists that salvation is by grace, through faith: '. . . *not* by works' (Eph. 2:8–9). The other claims that we are justified by what we *do*, '. . . and not by faith alone' (Jas. 2:24). Here is my attempt to harmonise these views . . .

Men and women have died for their passionate views on this controversy – it was one of the major issues which split Christendom into Catholic and Protestant during the sixteenth century Reformation. More recently ARCIC (formal discussions between Roman Catholics and Anglicans) has addressed this question in a more peaceful atmosphere!

It seems to me that the key is to be found in asking: which false views were the apostles combating? Paul was facing the danger of *spiritual pride*. There were those in the Church who thought that salvation was by self-effort rather than through grace and forgiveness. This played into the hands of those with strong self-discipline. James was facing the problem of *spiritual laziness*. Some people in the Church said, 'God has saved me, so why should I bother?'

Both apostles agree that faith properly understood is *dynamic*. It results in a trusting attitude; it also demands that we love and serve in Jesus' name and in his strength. The tension is resolved in Galatians 5:6, 'The only thing that counts is faith expressing itself through love.'

Both emphases can be found in the teaching of Jesus. He calls us to strenuous discipleship. And he invites 'all who are weary and burdened' to receive 'rest for your souls' (Matt. 11:28–29). Jesus taught the doctrine of justification by faith in a famous parable (Luke 18:14).

MEDITATION AND PRAYER

Read this passage by David Jenkins, Bishop of Durham:

As I have gone on developing experiences and impressions and feelings and glimpses of God as the power who is in all things and through all things and beyond all things and on the other side of all things, I have come more and more to feel that one way of picturing God is to think of him as an artist. A passionate, compassionate and infinitely patient artist.

Sit quietly while the leader speaks the following titles for God into the silence, at one minute intervals: Rock; Shepherd; King; Father.

Lord, you are our Rock – help us to build our lives upon a sure foundation.

Lord you are our Shepherd – help us to recognise your guidance and care in our daily lives.

Lord, you are our King – give us grace to obey.

Lord, you are our Father – we pray for all who know you not, or who love you not, or who by disobedience have grieved your heart of love.

Especially we pray for . . . Amen.

Father of all, we give you thanks and praise, that when we were still far off you met us in your Son and brought us home. (ASB)

Homework?

St Bernard speaks of our need to 'chew and masticate' words from the Bible. On Page 42 we considered some words used to describe God in the Psalms. You might care to spend time extending this list? Then take one picture each day and quietly meditate upon its meaning for your life – 'dissolving' it in your mind, rather as you might suck a peppermint.

I Believe in Jesus Christ . . . Born of the Virgin Mary

The word became flesh and made his dwelling among us (John 1:14).

He is the image of the invisible God, the firstborn over all creation (Col. 1:15).

When I saw him, I fell at his feet as though dead (Rev. 1:17)

GETTING STARTED

The great theologian Karl Barth visited America. He lectured at a seminary and a student asked, 'Dr Barth, what is the greatest thought that ever passed through your mind?' This question seemed to defeat him and he paused for a long time. How could this man, who wrote such long books, possibly sum it all up in a sentence or two? At last the professor looked up, and spoke with great sincerity:

> Jesus loves me! This I know,
> For the Bible tells me so.

That simple chorus apparently has significance in China too. I am told that during the dark years of the cultural revolution, a coded message came out of mainland China. It said 'the "this-I-know people" are alive and well.' It was a message from the Church.

* * *

Here is a young man who was born in an obscure village, the child of a peasant woman. He worked in a carpenter's shop until he was thirty, and then for three years he was an itinerant preacher. He never wrote a book. He never held an office . . . Nineteen centuries have come and gone and today he is the central figure of the human race. All the armies that ever marched, all the navies that ever sailed, all the parliaments that ever sat, all the kings that ever reigned, put together, have not affected [human] life as has that one solitary figure. WHY? (*Anon.*)

SETTING IT OUT

A local radio station ran a series of programmes about Jesus entitled *The Man Who Cut History in Half.* (Now an Epworth paperback by Frank Pagden.) That sums it up. To honour great saints we set aside one day each year. To honour Jesus, we divide history into BC and AD. His significance is immense; incomparable. As the American essayist R. W. Emerson put it, the name of Jesus '. . . is not so much written, as ploughed, into the history of the world.'

To play the numbers game (no guide to truth but a guide to significance), Jesus has more followers in the modern world than any other figure.

> None of the great founders of religions lived in so restricted an area. None lived for such a terribly short time. None died so young. And yet how great his influence has been . . . Numerically, Christianity is well ahead of all world religions. (*Professor Hans Küng*)

The incomparable significance of Jesus is widely acknowledged – and not only by Christians, as we shall see. But his significance for Christians is total. As the writer to the Hebrews put it, 'Let us keep our eyes fixed on Jesus, on whom our faith depends from beginning to end' (Heb. 12:2 Good News Bible).

Christianity finds its focus, *not* in a set of ideas or precepts or rules – but in a person and in a relationship. In this, Christianity differs from most other faiths.

Islam, for example. Christians and Muslims have a great deal in common. Both believe in one God; both believe that God has revealed his purposes for the world in a book; both honour one man as having supreme importance in that revelation. But Muslims do not worship Muhammad. And they dislike being called Muhammadans because this puts too much emphasis on the Prophet.

In contrast, the disciples of Jesus rejoice that the word Christian links them so closely with their Founder, whom they honour as prophet and teacher – and worship as Lord and God.

PROBING THE MEANING

Christianity is a very fishy story! The first disciples were fishermen, and the Greek word for fish (Ichthus) has great significance. In Greek, each letter points to something special about Jesus.

I	Iesous	Jesus
Ch	Christos	Christ
Th	Theou	Of God
U	(H)uios	Son
S	Soter	Saviour

In the Bible, Jesus is given numerous titles. The Apostles' Creed picks up a few of these and we shall examine them in turn: 'I believe in *Jesus Christ* his *only Son* our *Lord*.'

1. *Jesus*. This is the Greek form of a common Hebrew name: Joshua. But after Jesus of Nazareth it became less common – probably for two main reasons. Pious Jews were reluctant to burden their sons with such a despised and controversial name. Christians hesitated to call their sons by such an honoured name. It is a name with a meaning: 'God saves.' (Quite *literally*, Je-sus = God-saves.)

When naming his son Joshua, the devout Jew was recalling the history of his people – a history marked by the saving acts of God. When it came to the naming of Jesus, this saving activity was brought sharply into focus. 'You shall call his name Jesus', said the angel to Joseph, 'for he will save his people from their sins' (Matt. 1:21).

> To modern ears, talk about salvation from sin makes the coming of Jesus sound 'religious'. But properly understood, this is a concrete, practical business. It means: letting God get to work on my pride, my prejudices, my annoying habits, my greed, my lust, my laziness . . .

Even more important, it means allowing God to get to work on my whole outlook. 'Sin is a refusal to grow bigger' declared graffiti on the Cathedral of Notre Dame. We sin when we choose to remain safe, small and secure. God wants us to *grow*.

Most important of all: salvation involves surrendering ourselves to the love of God, rather than ignoring or rebelling against him.

2. *Christ*. The Old Testament was written in Hebrew; the New Testament in Greek. 'Christ' and 'Messiah' mean the same thing. 'Christ' is based on a Greek word; 'Messiah' is taken from Hebrew. Both words mean 'Anointed One' – anointed by God for a very special task, as kings were in Old Testament times.

At first it was a title: 'Jesus *the* Christ'. But because the title belonged so closely to the person, it became part of his name. Hence Jesus Christ. Just as John the Blacksmith at some point became John Smith.

3. *His only Son*. Jesus was very humble. He chose unimportant and unpopular people as friends. Yet his teaching contains mind-blowing claims. He claimed:

· to have a unique relationship with the Father

· to judge the world

· to forgive sins

· to fulfil the ancient covenant

· to be more significant than the all-important Sabbath

· to be more important than great Old Testament figures

· to speak words which will never pass away

Breath-taking assertions. Blasphemous if untrue – and way beyond the inventive powers of the early disciples. Yet these claims do not seem like boasting. It is rather like a modern tennis star who says – simply because it's *true* – 'I'm playing really well this season.'

These immense claims are woven quite naturally into Jesus' teaching about God and the way we should conduct our lives. Nevertheless, they raise enormous questions. They press us to decide whether Jesus was crazy, or wicked, or true. For only three kinds of people could make such claims.

· A wildly unbalanced person with false ideas about himself

· A liar who wants to impress people

· The one person of whom those claims are true.

There is no fourth possibility. We cannot deny that Jesus' view of himself and his mission is correct, and in the next breath speak of him as a great man and a fine teacher. If we refuse to accept his own estimate of himself, the alternatives are much harder than this.

> I see no escape from the dilemma: either Jesus is fraudulent or his claim is true: either we judge him for being terribly amiss, or we let him judge us. (*Lord Ramsey.*)

The question which confronts us from the Gospels is stark. Was Jesus insane – falsely believing himself to be divine? Was he a blasphemous impostor – merely pretending to be God's unique Son? Or was he really the person implied by his majestic claims?

The Creed is clear; Jesus is God's 'only Son'.

Of course, the New Testament calls *all* believers 'children of God' (1 John 3:1). But there is a crucial difference. *We* are children by adoption – chosen by God to be the little brothers and sisters of Jesus. *He* is God's 'only son', because he alone shares God's divine nature.

4. *Lord*. Perhaps the most remarkable title of all. With Thomas we often make it personal: Jesus is *my* Lord (John 20:28). This is a proper use of the title and Hans Küng gives a powerful definition of the word 'Christian' based upon it:

> A real Christian is not only a good and well-intentioned person but a man or woman for whom Jesus – not Caesar, not another god, not money, sex, power or pleasure, is Lord. (*Hans Küng*).

Important as this is, the phrase 'Jesus is Lord' means more – much more – than that. It refers to an objective truth. *For whether we acknowledge it or not, it remains true that Jesus is Lord – Lord of all creation.*

St Paul spells this out in his letter to the Philippians (2:6–11). He quotes an early Christian hymn which charts the downward path of Jesus. He who was in the form of God, humbly became a man. Then he consented to a grossly undignified death. Never has a downward path been so steep. But . . .

Because of his obedience, God raised and exalted him – so that 'at the name of Jesus every knee should bow'. In time – or rather in eternity – *all* will acknowledge that 'Jesus Christ is Lord' (Phil. 2:11).

The fact that this phrase comes in a letter by a *Jewish* Christian is totally unexpected. It is a fact which cries out for adequate explanation. For every Jew there was – and is – a great gulf fixed between the holy creator God and sinful human beings. They refused to place *any* man on the Godward side of that great divide. Many Jews died rather than acknowledge Caesar as divine.

Yet shortly after his death, the *Jewish* disciples of Jesus were calling him 'Lord'. In doing this, they placed him firmly on the *Godward* side of that unbridgeable gulf. For in their Scriptures, the term 'Lord' referred to God. It was an incredible shift in outlook; it can only be accounted for by the enormous impact made by Jesus.

This conclusion about Jesus forced itself upon them. It was beyond their imaginative powers to invent such an idea. Rather, the experiences underlying it were 'given', and they had to come to terms with them. Above all, this title points to the Resurrection of Jesus. For if Jesus is Lord over life and death — he is Lord indeed. All this was crystallised in the earliest Christian creed, which was very simple but very far-reaching: 'Jesus is Lord' (Rom. 10:9)

Yet the early Jewish disciples continued to believe in *one* God. Here we find the raw material from which the doctrine of the Trinity was quarried. But that is a story for another day!

The birth of JESUS

'I believe in Jesus Christ . . . who was conceived by the power of the Holy Spirit and born of the Virgin Mary.'

'Born of the Virgin Mary': Problem or Solution?

Christians believe that Jesus was a real man. He ate, he drank, he grew weary, he slept, he sweated, he smelt.

Christians also believe that Jesus is divine. When Thomas says, 'My Lord and my God' (John 20:28), we don't recoil in horror (as we would if such words were used about *absolutely anyone* else). Instead we say, 'Amen'.

In other words, Jesus is unique. So isn't a unique birth natural, too? In fact, the New Testament teaches that Jesus' *birth* was normal – but his *conception* wasn't. God's Spirit, not a human father, caused the baby to grow within his mother Mary.

Many Christians – I am one of these – rejoice in this as literal truth. Others deny that it should be taken literally – claiming that this puts the cart before the horse. What *really* happened (in their view) was something like this. The early Christians recognised the uniqueness of Jesus and they wanted to emphasise this. They knew of pagan stories about virgin births, so they invented stories about Jesus' unique conception. In this way they underlined his importance in God's plan for the world. By this means they hoped to convince Gentiles that Jesus was the unique Son of God.

Another explanation sometimes given is that Matthew pondered the Greek translation of Isaiah 7:14 – which speaks of a virgin giving birth – and applied this to Jesus. 'I think the early chapters of both Luke and Matthew are clearly stories that have been made up out of bits of the Old Testament and out of traditions about Jesus after he had been raised from the dead and that they knew for certain (the believers) that he was the Son of God – to show how special he was' (David Jenkins: Bishop of Durham).

Some go even further. They argue that the virgin birth originated in a false understanding of genetics in the ancient world. In their view, it is a stumbling block today because it distances Jesus from us. If Jesus was born of a virgin he 'is a diminished human being, not a complete human being, and certainly not like us in everything' (Dr John Toy, Chancellor of York Minster).

Whatever your viewpoint, here are some facts to chew:

1. Little is built upon the virgin birth in the Bible. The resurrection dominates the New Testament, but the virgin birth is stated explicitly only by Matthew and Luke. Even they do not dwell on its implications. They tell the story with few 'therefores' – *because* this happened, *therefore* this follows. (Scholars differ as to whether other NT writers refer obliquely to the virgin birth – and whether these references support or challenge it. See Mk 6:3; John 1:13, 1:45, 6:42, 8:41; Gal 4:4; Rom 1:3 [see Lk 3:23], 8:3, 9:6.)

2. The stories do not mean that the early Christians thought sex was wrong. Jews felt strongly about family life and believed sex within marriage was God-given. Later, some Christians gave sex a bad press – exalting celibacy and virginity as 'higher states'.

3. The reports about Jesus' unusual birth gave ammunition to the enemies of Jesus. Accusations that Jesus was illegitimate soon followed. If it was an invention designed to underline his significance, it misfired – in some quarters at least.

4. If the virgin birth didn't happen, the alternatives seem pretty stark. *Either* Mary conceived Jesus before her marriage – with Joseph, or an unknown man, as father. *Or* Jesus was conceived after Joseph and Mary married. In either case, the birth narratives in Matthew and Luke are imaginative inventions (designed to make a theological point, or to cover up the embarrassing truth). This raises serious questions

about the integrity of Mary and Joseph and/or Matthew and Luke.

5. The Jews knew – and despised – pagan myths about virgin births. That a Jewish writer like Matthew should invent such a story is hard to imagine. 'Little was more anathema to Jews than pagan myths of various sorts; and the idea that the very Jewish Matthew could have imitated some pagan myth in this way seems wholly unlikely' (Professor Keith Ward).

6. Modern Christians who deny that the virgin birth should be taken literally often stress three points:
   (a) They believe in the central truth to which the virgin birth bears witness i.e. the incarnation (that in Jesus, God became man).
   (b) We should not confuse a 'truth-carrying story' with the truth itself. All talk of lies and inventions is far too harsh; Matthew and Luke were expressing truth in subtle and imaginative ways.
   (c) To insist on the virgin birth as literal fact, is to introduce an unnecessary stumbling block to our evangelism. What counts is that people should put their faith in Jesus, not that they should cross t's and dot i's about secondary matters.

7. Others strongly disagree. In their view:
   (a) The virgin birth is not a secondary matter. To say that it is plays fast and loose with the Bible. Matthew and Luke were not writing 'truth-carrying stories'; they were recording events.
   (b) God is Creator: so why fuss about this particular creative act? 'What is impossible with men is possible with God' (Luke 18:27).
   (c) To treat the birth narratives in this way is far too

timid – over-sensitive to the spirit of the age. The Christian world view is committed to miracles; so why jib at this one? We need to remember Dean Inge's quip, that the Church which marries the spirit of the present age will find itself a widow in the next.

CORE QUESTIONS . . .

For Group Discussion and Individual Reflection

1. Draw up a check list of what you know about Jesus. (*As a group exercise, or individually.*)

Place and Date of birth ....

Nationality and Religion ....

Social Class ....

Father's occupation ....

Education ....

Occupation and Hobbies ....

Income ....

Friends/Associates ....
(rich, poor, weak, strong . . .)

Marital Status ....

Religious Views ....

Political outlook ....
(left/right wing, revolutionary . . . ?)

Duration of main work ....

Place and Cause of death ....

Present location of body ....

2. Imagine meeting a Buddhist visitor who knows very
little about Jesus. He asks you to outline three of the
most important themes in the teaching of Jesus.
What would you say? (Take a couple of minutes to
work this out individually or in pairs – then share
your ideas.) I have set out my own views in the
booklet *Jesus: The Verdict* (Lion 1990). For a
thorough treatment see *The Teaching of Jesus* by
Norman Anderson (Hodder 1983).

3. Select one parable of Jesus which takes us to the
heart of his teaching. Explain your choice. (My
choice is Luke 18:9–14.)

4. (a) Draw up a list of ten titles used for Jesus in the
New Testament. (If you cannot do this from
memory, scan St John's Gospel for a plentiful
supply.)
(b) Discuss the significance of five of these for life
today.
(c) Use the other five – one per day – for meditation
during the coming week.

5. A debate in General Synod in the spring of 1990
acknowledged that some Church of England bishops
don't accept the virgin birth as literal truth. Some
members of the Synod wanted bishops who think
like this to resign. Others argued that what *really*
matters is that in Jesus God became man. In their
view, to press belief in the virgin birth raises an
unnecessary stumbling block to evangelism.

What do you feel about all this?

BIBLE STUDY   Read these words by Provost David L. Edwards:

> Normally we read as quickly as possible, because we are reading newspapers, light fiction, etc. Or when we are studying a subject, we read as critically as possible. For a change, try reading suitable parts of the Bible as lovingly as possible — lingering over the scene, noticing every detail as if you had been there, asking what it shows you of God. Such 'meditation' on the Bible supplies a solid basis for prayer — and life. When you have got clearer in your mind the reality of God, coming to you in Jesus, stepping out of the pages of the Bible, you will find it easier to put together the jigsaw of your life.

Now read Matthew 9:9–13 and 9:18–31. Discuss how you might apply one of these episodes to your life, as David Edwards suggests.

Homework?

You might care to do the same with Matthew 14:22–36. Please share your findings next week. Do you find this a helpful method of Bible study, prayer and meditation? If so, why not use it regularly?

. . . AND MORE QUESTIONS

Please read the note on page 32 entitled *Why More Questions* at this point.

6. I recall a conversation with a man who said, with total conviction: 'I take everything in the Bible quite literally.' Yet he owned a house, a car, and at least

two coats! Do you think Jesus intends us to take his teaching literally? Try these for a start:

- turn the other cheek (Matt. 5:39)
- forgive seventy times seven (Matt. 18:22)
- give everything away (Luke 12:33–34)
- hate your father and mother (Luke 14:26). (No wonder some modern versions tone this down!)

7. (a) Do you believe in the virgin birth? (or virginal conception to be pedantically accurate).
   (b) Many modern people find the virgin birth a stumbling block because they find miracles in general very difficult to accept. Do you?
   (c) What would you say to someone who challenges the fact that Jesus performed miracles?

8. An elderly church-goer said to me: 'Jesus means more to you than to me. For me it is God the Father who is really significant.'
   (a) Can you identify with that viewpoint?
   (b) Do you regard Jesus primarily as an ancient teacher, as an ever-present friend, as a distant figure in majesty, as . . .
   (c) Do modern Christians over-emphasise Jesus and the Holy Spirit? Is it (un)healthy that different believers should stress different Persons within the Trinity?
   (d) Do you involve Jesus in the big crises and joys of your life. How?
   (e) Do you involve Jesus in your daily, routine life? How?

9. How would you define 'Christian', given the fact that six out of the nine letters form the name 'Christ'?

10. Select one passage or quotation from this chapter for

comment – a passage which inspires/troubles/
annoys/encourages you or . . . (You may wish to do
this exercise for other chapters, too.)

BIBLE STUDY   Read John 1:9, John 14:6 and Acts 4:12.
Then consider these words of Archbishop George Carey:

Christianity makes the bold claim that Jesus Christ is so
incomparable that we meet God fully in Him . . .
Mainstream Christianity treats other religions with
respect and allows that God can be known, and is
known by men and women of non-Christian faiths . . .
But we cannot shift from the conviction that is as old as
the New Testament that God is revealed FULLY AND
FINALLY in the person of Jesus Christ.

Is he too harsh on other faiths?

Is he too easy on other faiths?

Do you agree with the Archbishop?

(See page 123 of *The Great God Robbery* by George
Carey for his full statement. I have discussed this issue in
Our God is Still Too Small: Hodder, Chapter 17.)

LONG TERM BIBLE STUDY   Work through the Gospels and
draw up a complete list of the titles given to Jesus. If you
are really ambitious, you might tackle the New Testament
letters and the Book of Revelation too. Definitely a task
for long winter evenings! If you do this, turn it into a
devotional exercise, 'savouring' each title – rather like
sipping a liqueur!

VIEWPOINTS . . . ON THE VIRGIN BIRTH

- **PREBENDARY MICHAEL SAWARD**   If Mary was not *Virgo Intacta*, then someone was lying somewhere.

- **BISHOP JOHN AUSTIN BAKER**   The virgin birth is significant because it is related to the Christian belief that in Jesus God himself is present, living a human life . . . the entry of God into the world has got to be miraculous whichever way it happened.

- **BISHOP JOHN ROBINSON**   The early Christians were not convinced that Jesus was the Son of God because of anything that happened when he was born. They were convinced *by what they saw in him*. He showed them a new kind of living, a new kind of loving, quite out of this world . . . This is what the virgin birth is saying. And this is a truth about him which I firmly believe. With regard to the biological details, I am prepared to keep an open mind. Nothing for me depends upon them.

- **PROFESSOR KEITH WARD**   The strongest argument for the veracity of these accounts [of the virgin birth] is that it is very hard to see why they should have been invented, when they would have been so shocking to Jewish ears . . . What could have been their motive, except to say that is was true?

- **THE CHURCH OF ENGLAND BISHOPS**   The central miracle, the heart of the Christian understanding of God, is the Incarnation itself . . . But all of us accept . . . that the belief that our Lord was conceived in the womb of Mary by the creative power of God the Holy Spirit without the intervention of a human father can be held with full intellectual integrity.

. . . that only this belief, enshrined in the Creeds, can claim to be the teaching of the universal Church

. . . that in God Christ has taken the initiative for our salvation by uniting our human nature with himself, so bringing into being a new humanity (*The Nature of Christian Belief*; Church House Publishing, 1986).

VIEWPOINTS . . . ON JESUS

- **MOTHER TERESA** Evangelism means to carry Jesus in your heart and to give the presence of Jesus to someone else . . .

- **ARCHBISHOP MICHAEL RAMSEY** Jesus is divine; that is the faith of Christendom. But there is a corollary to it: God is Christlike.

- **BISHOP HUGH MONTEFIORE** Good News from Jesus was that God's Kingdom was dawning, with its marks of love, joy, peace, justice and goodness . . . By his death and resurrection he showed he was not merely the bearer of the Kingdom, but himself the King.

- **SADHU SUNDAR SINGH** Without Christ I was like a fish out of water. With Christ I am in the ocean of love.

- **DOROTHY L. SAYERS** You cannot have Christian principles without Christ.

- **THOMAS CARLYLE** If Jesus Christ were to come today people would not crucify him. They would ask him to dinner and hear what he had to say, and make fun of it.

- **POPE JOHN XXIII** When men are animated by the love of Christ they feel united, and the needs, sufferings and joys of others are felt as their own.

- **DR COLIN MORRIS** Because we were alienated from Reality and couldn't find our way back, Reality burst into our fevered world of illusion in the person of Jesus.

- **C. S. LEWIS** The historical difficulty of giving for the life, sayings and influence of Jesus any explanation that is not harder than the Christian explanation, is very great.

- **ARCHBISHOP GEORGE CAREY** The word 'church' seems so static, representing a building . . . The idea of movement – the Jesus movement – is much more dynamic.

- **EDWARD HARMAN** (Borford Church, 1569) Christ it is that sustains you and calls you to dwell with him. Laugh at the threats of disease, care not for the dark grave, and go forth at Christ's summons, for Christ will be to each man, a kingdom, a light, a life, a crown.

- **PROFESSOR SIR NORMAN ANDERSON** The teaching of Jesus stands on an Everest alone. No other teaching has had the same impact and influence, in countless lives and diverse cultures. No other teaching has provoked so much change, or stirred up so much debate.

- **JOHN STOTT** A man who loves his wife will love her letters and her photographs because they speak to him of her. So if we love the Lord Jesus we shall love the Bible because it speaks to us of him.

- **DOSTOYEVSKY** I believe there is no one lovelier, deeper, more sympathetic and more perfect than Jesus.

- **GANDHI** (a Hindu) I believe that he belongs . . . to the entire world.

- **MARTIN BUBER** (a Jew) . . . a great place belongs to him in Israel's history of faith. This place cannot be described by any of the usual categories.

- **MILAN MACHOVEC** (a Communist) Jesus set the world on fire.

MEDITATION AND PRAYER

Ask different members to read Matthew 11:25–30 and Revelation 5:12–14.

He was too great for his disciples . . . Is it any wonder that to this day this Galilean is too much for our small hearts? (H. G. Wells).

Sit in an attitude of prayer and ask one member of the group to read out these titles at one minute intervals:

Light of the world

Bread of life

Lamb of God

Teacher.

In the silence apply them to your own life and to our world.

Thanks be to you, my Lord Jesus Christ, for all the benefits which you have given me, for all the pains and insults which you have borne for me. O most merciful Redeemer, Friend and Brother: may I know you more clearly, love you more dearly, and follow you more nearly, day by day. Amen.
(The prayer of St Richard of Chichester: 1197–1253.)

He . . . was Crucified

He suffered . . . under Pontius Pilate, was crucified, died, and was buried . . . I believe in the forgiveness of sins (Apostles' Creed).

Then they led him out to crucify him (Mark 15:20) . . . you who once were far away have been brought near through the blood of Christ (Eph. 2:13).

GETTING STARTED

Wendy, her husband John and their two young daughters toured France during the summer holidays. They visited a Church which contained several ornaments and Christian symbols. Wendy's eyes were drawn to the cross.

She had links with the Church as a child but had drifted away, although she still believed in God. As she looked at the tortured figure on the crucifix, she was overwhelmed with a sense of unworthiness and ingratitude. 'To think that he died for *me*, and I spend my life ignoring *him*.'

She wept.

From that moment, Wendy took every opportunity to visit church buildings. At each place the story was repeated: the sorrow, the joy, the tears. Gratitude gradually overcame guilt and she simply wanted to stand, to kneel, to look, to think, and to pray.

Wendy's children seemed to understand that something very significant and holy was happening. They did not clamour for attention but gave time and space for her to be on her own. Still the tears flowed and sunglasses became necessary even in the dark churches – to hide the tears and the embarrassment.

Wendy arrived home with a new determination to follow the Christ whom she had rediscovered on that holiday.

As I listened to her moving story, it struck me again that in a world where we rightly want to understand, to quantify, to tie down and to measure, there are some things which can only be received and responded to.

* * *

Suppose a farmhand set fire to his master's barn. The man is liable for the damages with all that he has. The master could take everything the servant has. But the master does nothing of the sort, takes nothing away. He rather says to the faithless servant, 'I will take everything upon myself; I will pay everything.' And then the servant opens his eyes in amazement; for he sees what a good master he has.

God dealt with us in this way through Jesus Christ. He has taken everything upon Himself; He has Himself borne the curse of sin that we should have carried. Apart from the cross on Golgotha we should know neither our condition nor the boundlessness of God's love. Jesus reveals both us and God on the cross. And by that act He accomplishes the greatest thing possible: He brings men back again to God.

(Abridged from *Our Faith* by Emil Brunner (SCM).)

SETTING IT OUT

Christianity is about concepts and ideas – ideas like love, forgiveness and judgement. But the ideas are earthed in life and history. So the Apostles' Creed is mainly about *events*; things which *happened* in a certain place at a particular time. This week's title makes this very clear. It takes us to the heart and centre of our faith.

Jesus suffered – and the Creed tells us *when*. He died when Pontius Pilate was Procurator in Palestine. Poor Pontius Pilate. Remembered weekly by millions for an act of compromise – and for the most famous washing incident in all history.

St Luke does much the same thing in his Gospel. At one point he tells us that the word of God came to John the Baptist, in the wilderness (Luke 3:1,2). To help the reader fix the point in time, he gives a list of famous men who were ruling then.

How time changes perspectives! Tiberius Caesar with his world strategy; King Herod with his magnificent building plans; Pontius Pilate with his personal ambitions and fears. These were the famous household names of their day. But were it not for the fact that they ruled when John the Baptist preached in the wilderness, and when Jesus was born in Bethlehem or died on Calvary, they would be known only to a handful of professional historians.

In most biographies, the subject's death is given a page or two. In contrast, the Gospels give the death of Jesus enormous significance. St Mark's Gospel – the shortest and probably the earliest – devotes one third of its material to the events surrounding the crucifixion. Why?

To probe this question, let's consider a more recent event:

(a) *A loving action.* On 25th May 1971, a terrorist dumped a bomb in the hall of a Police Station in Belfast. Sergeant Michael Willetts of the Parachute Regiment entered the hall and held the door open to allow adults and children to escape. He then stood in the doorway, shielding those taking cover. The immense blast killed him.

Michael was awarded the George Cross for his bravery. The official register states: 'By this considered act of bravery Sergeant Willetts risked – and lost – his life for those of the adults and children.'

That incident illustrates one of the answers which the New Testament gives to the question: Why is the death of Christ so important? *It illustrates the love of God.* That man proved his concern for his neighbours by dying for them. God proved his care for us by sending his Son. His Son proved his love for us by giving his life.

Rather than using his power to dominate, Jesus chose to submit to the worst that we could do. So the power of God is seen in symbols of weakness – in a borrowed manger and a wooden cross. Here is power kept in check; power handed over; power utterly controlled by love. 'God so loved the world that he gave his one and only Son . . .' (John 3:16)

But all this leads to a further question. In what sense did Christ die for us? That soldier saved his friends in a literal, physical sense. The death of Jesus works at a less obvious, yet much more profound level. How can his death *then*, save us *now*?

(b) *A significant contrast* To explore this question, we will visit Gaul during the second century. Blandina was a slave and a Christian. She had the misfortune to live in Lyons in AD 177 when the authorities tried to stamp out the Church. The job was straightforward. They had to persuade the Christians to disown their God and swear by pagan idols. The early historian Eusebius recorded the events of those days. The believers were mocked and tortured in an arena. Blandina, he reported, wore out her tormentors with her endurance. So they put her back in prison.

Later they brought her into the arena again, with a fifteen-year-old boy called Ponticus. After he had been killed, they put Blandina in a basket and presented her to a bull. 'And so,' wrote Eusebius, 'she travelled herself along the same path of conflicts as they [her fellow Christians] did, and hastened to them, rejoicing and exulting in her departure.'

The peace and serenity – and sense of the *presence* of God – displayed by Blandina, is characteristic of the Christian martyrs since the death of Stephen (Acts 7:54–60). They showed a deep – even joyful – sense of God's presence. *This is in sharp contrast with the death of Jesus.*

We find there a *lack* of serenity: he was 'in anguish of spirit'. We find there a *lack* of peace: 'Father, if it be your will, take this cup from me.' We find there a *lack* of a sense of the presence of God: 'My God, my God, why have you forsaken me?'

For those who died for Christ – a constant sense of the presence of God. For Jesus as he died – a sense of abandonment by God, and of utter loneliness.

The martyrs faced death willingly: Jesus shrank from it.

Jesus wasn't less brave than those who followed him. No. He could have turned north – back to Galilee and safety. Instead, 'Jesus resolutely set out for Jerusalem' (Luke 9:51). Resolutely, because he knew what awaited him there. In every century, Christian martyrs have drawn inspiration from his courage.

The fact remains: Jesus' death was marked by anguish, while many of his followers faced death with serenity. This surprising difference presents us with a puzzle. It is a puzzle to which the New Testament gives a solution. The answer given there is this: for Jesus, there was an *extra factor*.

The martyrs suffered physically. Jesus suffered physically – and spiritually. They bore *pain* for him. He bore *sin* for them.

PROBING THE MEANING

The New Testament reveals the meaning of Christ's death, by treating it as a diamond whose beauty is best seen by shafts of light from various directions. So having approached this vital subject from one angle, we shall look at it from another – by probing six key Bible words.

> The writers of the New Testament ransacked language to find some way of conveying the sense of what had happened to Jesus on Calvary. They used the jargon of the law courts and the slave galleys and the slaughter house to get across the meaning of his death . . . (*Dr Colin Morris*)

1. MEDIATOR. 'For there is one God and one mediator between God and men, the man Christ Jesus, who gave himself as a ransom for all' (1 Tim. 2:5). We cut ourselves off from other people when we turn our backs on them — or when we refuse to have anything to do with them at anything but a superficial level. The Bible makes it clear that we have cut ourselves off from God by our disobedience and indifference. To bring two separated parties together, a mediator or 'trouble-shooter' is sometimes required. But this is a dangerous job, for it might mean getting involved in the dispute — like Terry Waite.

This is just what Jesus did. He came to be the mediator between humanity and God. To end this 'cold war' he had to get involved in it. In order to destroy the dark cloud which had come between us and God through our rebellion, Jesus had to enter that cloud.

He did this on the cross. He removed the barrier by taking it upon himself. Just *how* Jesus did this is something which we cannot fully understand. But we do find clues in his teaching. And this great truth is explored at many other points in the New Testament.

The fact *that* he did this is shown by his own deep sense of the absence of God — in complete contrast to the rest of his life. That he did this *successfully* is shown by the words which he uttered from the cross. 'It is accomplished!' (John 19:30 REB). His success was demonstrated by a powerful sign: the veil in the temple was torn from top to bottom (Mark 15:38). That curtain stood as a symbol of the barrier between the Holy God and his sinful people. When Jesus died on Calvary, the symbol of separation was destroyed.

It was because of this that those who suffered for Jesus experienced such a deep sense of the *presence* of God. For them the cloud had disappeared.

It is in the Cross that the human predicament – our disharmony with God, and with other people – finds its solution. It is for this reason that Baptism and Holy Communion are so important – for they focus on the cross. They declare the good news of reconciliation and sins forgiven.

2. EXAMPLE. The death of Jesus is the supreme demonstration of the love of God. And it is the place where our relationship with God can be restored. But these answers – great as they are – do not exhaust its meaning.

The New Testament makes it clear that there is another great answer to the question, 'Why did Jesus die?' *He died as our example* (1 Pet. 2:21). The cross of Christ has to be *applied*, not merely *observed*. 'If anyone would come after me, he must deny himself and take up his cross . . .' (Mark 8:34) said Jesus.

He died *for* us; he asked us to die *with* him. For some, this means literal martyrdom. For all, it means a sort of death. It means:

- upholding Christian standards in a world which rejects those standards.

- witnessing to Christ in a world which is indifferent to him.

- showing love, when it would be much easier to be indifferent.

- forgiving when it would be much more 'natural' to seek revenge.

Even this does not complete the story. The death of Jesus can never be understood apart from the resurrection – for Jesus was too good and too great to be held by death. He died on the cross, only to rise again.

This is always the pattern. It is by dying with Christ that we find life. It is in losing ourselves that we find ourselves. What we throw away, we receive back in abundance. God is no man's debtor.

All this talk about the Cross may seem gloomy and dismal. But in the Bible, words like death, crucifixion and Calvary are always found in the company of other words. Words like life, resurrection and hope. The cross is a gateway to life, not the end of a track.

But there can be no fooling with Christ. A gold cross on a chain may be pretty. A silver cross in a church may look beautiful. The prototype was rough, and ugly, and stained with blood and smeared with sweat.

A man gasping for breath on a gallows will not allow a superficial response. Either we accept his invitation to follow, or we do not. But let us be clear. If we follow, it must be on *his* terms, not ours.

---

3. ATONEMENT. Literally, at-one-ment. The Christian Gospel is about reconciliation (2 Cor. 5:19,20). The death of Jesus built bridges across apparently unbridge-able gaps. To change the picture, it knocked down two dividing walls (Eph. 2:14):

· between the Holy God and his sinful children

· between Jews and Gentiles

Elsewhere the new Testament is even bolder. Christ's

death brings together *all* things previously fragmented. Nature itself will be redeemed (Col. 1:20; Rom. 8:20–22).

The idea of atonement runs throughout the Bible. In the Old Testament we find an elaborate set of rituals based on the tabernacle and temple. These found their focus in animal sacrifices. Those ancient practices have no practical significance for Christians today; but they do loudly declare two things which still need to be heard:

· *God is holy*   The Israelites must not get 'chummy' with their God. As his creatures – and sinful creatures at that – they needed to prepare themselves very carefully before approaching him.

· *Sin is serious*   God will not wink at sin; he takes it very seriously indeed. Sin can only be covered by sacrifice. But – as the letter to the Hebrews makes clear – animal sacrifices were not enough. They were but a shadow of the Real Thing which was yet to come.

At Calvary Jesus became the one perfect sacrifice *and* the one true High Priest. The way back to God is open. We can come to him with confidence (Heb. 10:19, Eph. 3:12). *Boldness* is different from *chumminess*. Jesus tells us to trust God, to love God – and to fear and obey God.

4. RANSOM/REDEEM. 'For even the Son of Man did not come to be served, but to serve, and to give his life as a ransom for many' (Mark 10:45).

The Bible enthuses about the great dignity of human beings. We are made in the very image of God. It also speaks about the deep degradation of human nature. 'Light has come into the world, but men loved darkness instead of light because their deeds were evil' (John 3:19).

It was human pride which opposed Jesus; it was human greed which betrayed Jesus; it was human sin which convicted Jesus. (*Human* sin, not Jewish sin or Roman sin. Jews and Romans just happened to be centre stage at the time. 'Were you there when they crucified my Lord?' asks the old Negro spiritual. Yes, I was: standing near the back of the crowd; uncertain which way to jump; afraid to commit myself; frightened for my own skin.)

> When Jesus died, the land was covered in daytime darkness. It was as though heaven itself was saying: *this* is the most terrible day of all. The Son of God is killed by the sons of men. But that dreadful day has enormous significance. So we call it *Good* Friday.

For God took those evil events and attitudes and used them as raw material from which to quarry our salvation. Which is why Jesus referred to his death as a 'ransom'. A slave in the ancient world could be redeemed – set free – by a ransom price paid on his behalf. In the same way we can be set free – by all that Jesus did for us on the cross. It is by this means, and no other, that we are redeemed from sin and fear and death.

Just *how* his death can do this for us is a deep mystery – a mystery which has brought light and understanding to countless lives. The New Testament explores this mystery and we glimpse the mind and ways of God. But we cannot fully understand the meaning of Jesus' death – nor what it cost his Father to give him up for us in this way.

5. COVENANT is another key Bible word which is woven through both Testaments. (Indeed, 'covenant' means 'testament'.) This great word reminds us of God's

love for his world, and his commitment to us. Throughout the Old Testament, he renewed and reinforced his covenant with individuals (Noah, Abraham, Moses, David) and with the whole nation. But the Israelites rejected their God and broke their side of 'the agreement'.

So the prophets looked forward with longing to a new era and a new covenant – a covenant with love and forgiveness at its centre, and the Holy Spirit as its seal. Jeremiah, for example, six hundred years before Jesus, when Jerusalem was under siege, spoke bold words of glorious hope. '"The time is coming" declares the Lord, "when I will make a new covenant with the house of Israel and with the house of Judah"' (Jer. 31:31).

At the Last Supper Jesus picked up this theme. He took bread, gave thanks and broke it. Then he took wine and declared, 'This is my blood of the covenant, which is poured out for many for the forgiveness of sins' (Matt. 26:28). In doing so, he made it clear that:

• his own death was central to this new covenant

• forgiveness of sins was the main outcome of this new covenant

Shortly after that meal, Jesus was captured, tried and crucified. His body was broken. His life was poured out like wine, for you and for me.

6. SERVANT. The prophet Isaiah wrote about the Servant of the Lord. He was the *suffering* Servant. The earliest Christians made the connection: Jesus was that Servant. Indeed, Jesus saw his own ministry like that. 'The Son of Man . . . came *to serve*' (Mark 10:45). Amazing, humbling and true.

This Servant identified himself with the poor, the powerless, the stranger, the marginalised. 'Whatever you did for one of the least of these brothers of mine, you did for me' (Matt. 25:40).

Where is God when we suffer? Where was he in the concentration camps? Where is he in the shanty towns? Where was he in the Romanian orphanages? (nearly five hundred children, and not a single bar of soap).

Where is God? He is there. In the gas chamber; drinking the foul water; dirty and runny-nosed.

'God was in Christ reconciling the world to himself' (2 Cor. 5:19, RSV). It was God in Christ who died in the hot sun. It was God in Christ who hung naked and exposed. It was God in Christ who was too helpless even to brush away the flies. This is the message of the cross.

A few years ago I was interested in buying a picture based on a Russian icon. As proceeds from the sale would help Christians in Eastern Europe, and as I am moved by some Russian art, it seemed a happy combination. Then I read the description. The print showed Jesus in Glory. He was strong and serene – apparently above, and untouched by, the sufferings of the world.

I did not buy that picture, after all. No doubt it conveyed deep truths about the vindication and glorification of Jesus. But it seemed to me to distort the meaning of the cross. Jesus is no mere spectator of the anguish of the world. He understands it *from the inside*.

All this leads us to a gospel of hope and joy. We are not on our own in a cold, heartless universe. At the centre of all things is the crucified God – who brings life out of death.

We find hope even in the darkest moment of the Cross. 'My God, my God, why have you forsaken me?' cried Jesus. He was quoting the opening line of Psalm 22. As Rabbi Hugo Gryn points out, the opening line of a Psalm represents the *whole Psalm* to a devout Jew. And Psalm 22 breathes confidence and faith. Even the desolation is shot through with hope.

The poor will eat and be satisfied;
They who seek the Lord will praise him (Ps 22:26).

CORE QUESTIONS . . .

For Group Discussion and Individual Reflection

1. The Gospels record seven sayings of Jesus from the cross. Brainstorm your group to see how many you can remember. Then look them up and write them down on one sheet of paper: (three in Luke; three in John; one in Matthew and Mark).

   (a) What do they tell us about Jesus?
   (b) Are they only of historical interest – or do they speak to us about life in the modern world? If so, how?
   (c) Perhaps memorise these seven sayings for use as a devotional aid – bringing them to mind from time to time.

2. The New Testament links our forgiveness with the death of Jesus. This is made very clear in Holy Communion when we recall the words of Jesus: 'Drink this, all of you; this is my blood of the new covenant, which is shed for you and for many

for the forgiveness of sins' (ASB). Imagine two conversations:

(a) with someone who feels that she cannot attend Holy Communion because she feels unworthy. What would you say?

(b) with an enquirer who asks you to describe your inner experiences when you receive Holy Communion. How do you feel? What goes through your mind? Do you concentrate? On what? Does it matter? Any devices which help you?

3. I spoke recently with a woman whose child had died. One saying of Jesus had helped her more than any other in her suffering. It wasn't his affirmation of victory over death ('I am the Resurrection and the Life'). It wasn't his promise of strength ('I am with you always'). It was his cry of dereliction: 'My God, my God, why have you forsaken me?'

(a) How can such a cry bring comfort?

(b) Do you know other people who feel this way?

4. On the cross Jesus cried out, 'Father forgive them . . .' He requires this same attitude from his followers, e.g. in the Lord's Prayer.

(a) Share with other group members your biggest struggle with forgiveness:
   – In giving it
   – In asking for it – from God or other people
   – In receiving it – from God or other people

(b) If someone said, 'My biggest problem is to forgive myself' or 'I find it hard to forgive God'; what would you say to them?

5. Artists often paint people in modern dress at Calvary. In this way they declare that the cross belongs to the *whole* of life – it must not be captured and tamed by religion, nor trapped in history.

   (a) Any comments on modern paintings of the cross?

   (b) Discuss Lord Macleod's assertion on page 98.

... AND MORE QUESTIONS

Please read the note in chapter 1 entitled *Why More Questions* at this point.

6. *When I survey the wondrous cross*
   On which the Prince of glory died,
   My richest gain I count but loss,
   And pour contempt on all my pride.

   (a) Do these words speak to you?

   (b) Do other hymns about the death of Jesus? Which, and how?

7. Read Mark 8:34–38.

   (a) What might it mean for Christians in repressive countries to 'take up the cross and follow him'?

   (b) What might this phrase mean for us?

8. St Luke adds the words 'every day' to the phrase, 'Take up your cross'. Yet in the Roman Empire you never carried your cross more than once. St Paul declared 'I die daily' – an obvious impossibility inside or outside the Roman Empire.

   (a) Are these paradoxes confusing or helpful?

   (b) What do they mean for you and me?

9. In the light of the death of Jesus, discuss

   (a) holiness
   (b) Jesus' instruction to love God and to fear God.

10. Do you find the use of words and phrases such as
    'Salvation', 'Atonement', 'Washed in the blood of
    the lamb', helpful or difficult? Should churches en-
    courage more discussion and explanation of difficult
    words? Or use simpler words?

11. 'Father forgive them . . .' A vicar was clubbed un-
    conscious and his daughter was raped. He said that
    he fully forgave the attackers but hoped that they
    would get very stiff prison sentences.

    (a) Does his attitude contain a contradiction?
    (b) Is it possible – or even right – for us to forgive
        someone for a hurt done to someone else?
    (c) How can we come to terms with the long-term
        damage which we have caused someone else –
        even if they have forgiven us?

12. If asked, 'how can Jesus' death *then*, save us *now*?'
    What would you say?

13. Bishop Stephen Neill explained the Hindu principle
    of *Karma*. Do well and your next life will be on a
    higher level – and vice versa. Karma says, 'You sin
    . . . you pay'. Christ says, 'You sin . . . I pay'. Karma
    has logic and nobility. Indeed it has been argued that
    forgiveness is immoral.

    (a) Is Karma noble and forgiveness weak?
    (b) Do you really want a child murderer to be
        forgiven?

    (c) Where would *we* be if Karma ruled instead of forgiveness?

14. Discuss any point in this chapter (including *Viewpoints*) which puzzles, helps, depresses or inspires you.

15. The cross centres on reconciliation – with God, neighbour and nature. A door has been opened and we are invited to go through. Do you need to take any specific action with a particular neighbour? Have you ever made *your* peace with God in a deeply personal way? (This question may be too sensitive for group discussion – but some members may welcome an opportunity to share their problems, worries and joys.)

Homework

The cross declares: 'You have deep and desperate needs.' It rebukes our pride and self-sufficiency. It insists that we come humbly and kneel quietly. Compose a devotional prayer to Jesus our crucified saviour. (For use in meetings, Services or magazines?)

VIEWPOINTS

· **ANTHONY HARVEY**   'Jesus was crucified under Pontius Pilate.' There is no single fact about the ancient world that is better attested than this.

· **STUDDERT KENNEDY**

· When Jesus came to Golgotha they hanged him on a tree,
   They drove great nails through hands and feet, and made a Calvary;

They crowned him with a crown of thorns, red were
    his wounds and deep,
For those were crude and cruel days, and human
    flesh was cheap.

When Jesus came to Birmingham they simply passed
    him by,
They never hurt a hair of him, they only let him die;
For men had grown more tender, and they would not
    give him pain,
They only just passed down the street, and left him in
    the rain.

Still Jesus cried, 'Forgive them, for they know not
    what they do,'
And still it rained the wintry rain that drenched him
    through and through;
The crowds went home and left the streets without a
    soul to see,
And Jesus crouched against a wall and cried for
    Calvary.

· OCTAVIUS WINSLOW   Who delivered up Jesus to die?
Not Judas, for money; not Pilate, for fear; not the Jews,
for envy; – but the Father, for love!

· JOHN STOTT   On the human level, Judas gave him up to
the priests . . . But on the divine level, the Father gave
him up, and he gave himself up, to die for us.

· DESMOND TUTU   That is tremendous stuff – that is the
Good News. Whilst we were yet sinners, says St Paul,
Christ died for us. God did not wait until we were die-
able, for He could have waited till the cows came
home.

- **LORD MACLEOD**   I am recovering the claim that Jesus was not crucified in a cathedral between two candles, but on a cross between two thieves . . . at the kind of place where cynics talk smut, and thieves curse, and soldiers gamble. Because this is where he died. And this is what he died about. And that is where churchmen ought to be, and what churchmen should be about.

- **JOHN POLKINGHORNE**   Why was not Jesus' life sufficient to reconcile us to God? . . . It is hard to forgive a real wrong; it is hard to accept the real forgiveness of a wrong. I think that this costliness of forgiveness is the clue to why the act of redemption had to involve the total surrender of death.

- **MOTHER TERESA**   When Jesus came into the world, he loved it so much that he gave his life for it. And what did he do? He made himself the Bread of Life. He became small, fragile and defenceless for us.

- **PROVOST DAVID L. EDWARDS**   By dying like that, Jesus has won the right to be 'our Lord'. The word 'lord' here means 'boss' . . . There are many ways of defining what a 'Christian' is. The best one is this: a Christian is one who takes his orders from Jesus Christ as Lord.

- **DR COLIN MORRIS**   In the suffering and death of Jesus, God himself was somehow fully present – sharing his sacrificial love for all his children.

- **IAN PETIT**   I only really began to understand the central truths of the Gospel after I had been a priest for many years . . . My life was not wicked, nor peppered with great sins, but it was full of *my* directing, *my* efforts, *my*

making myself holy. I needed to learn that that sort of
life has been dealt with by Christ's dying and rising.

- **BISHOP RICHARD HOLLOWAY**   Jesus belongs to the
  world, not to the Church. He died for all, not for a few.

- **ASB**   Christ crucified draw you to himself, to find in him
  a sure ground for faith, a firm support for hope, and the
  assurance of sins forgiven.

- **ELIZA DOOLITTLE**   Words, words, words. Don't talk of
  love. *Show me!*

MEDITATION AND PRAYER

In AD 156, old Bishop Polycarp of Smyrna stood in a
pagan stadium. He was challenged to deny Jesus Christ
and embrace the pagan gods. He declared; 'I have been
his servant for eighty-six years and he has never done me
any wrong. How then can I blaspheme my king who
saved me?' He was burnt to death.

If you and I were on trial for following Christ – would
there be enough evidence to convict us?

Read a passion hymn *or* Psalm 22 *or* Isaiah 53
Read aloud the Studdert Kennedy poem on pages 96–7

Lord Jesus, lamb of God who takes away the sin of the
world; bear our sins away. Lord Jesus, crucified
Saviour of the world, come into our hearts, into our
homes, into our churches and redeem us. Lord Jesus,
crucified prince of peace, rule in our lives, that we may
rise with you to glory. Amen.

On the Third Day He Rose Again

And if Christ has not been raised, your faith is futile (1 Cor. 15:17).

Surely I am with you always, to the very end of the age (Matt. 28:20).

GETTING STARTED

34% of British people do not know why Easter is celebrated (MORI poll: Easter 1991).

* * *

Three years after the Russian Revolution of 1917, a great anti-God rally was arranged in Kiev. The powerful orator Bukharin was sent from Moscow, and for an hour he demolished the Christian faith with argument, abuse, and ridicule.

At the end there was silence. Then questions were invited.

A man rose and asked to speak. He was a priest of the Russian Orthodox Church and he stood next to Bukharin, facing the people. He spoke three words: the ancient liturgical greeting used on Easter Sunday. 'Christ is Risen.'

At once, the entire assembly stood and gave the joyful response. 'He is risen indeed.' A devastating moment for an atheist politician, who made no reply. (Source: Bishop Lesslie Newbigin.)

SETTING IT OUT

Of course, this does not prove the resurrection. Indeed, Good Friday gives a dramatic reminder that majorities can be terribly wrong. So the question persists. Dead men don't rise; so why believe that this particular dead man did rise? The answer is to be found in the uniqueness of Jesus and in the power of God.

Jesus was too good and too great to be held by death. Having defeated sin on the cross, it was inevitable that he should go on to defeat sin's first cousin. But Jesus did not raise himself. The New Testament asserts that it was God the Father who raised Jesus from the dead. At the beginning of time, God created the universe out of nothing. Now he brings life out of death.

Easy to say but – for many people in the modern world – hard to believe. And for some people in the ancient world, too. At the end of St Luke's Gospel we read that 'they still did not believe it because of joy and amazement' (Luke 24.41). The disciples had visited the empty tomb; they had seen the risen Lord. Still they disbelieved. Not only because they were stubborn and disobedient; but because they were overwhelmed. It seemed too good to be true. They disbelieved . . . because of joy!

We modern Christians are so familiar with the idea of resurrection that we sometimes forget just how incredible it is. Jesus did not pretend to die. He really was *stone cold dead*. The Apostles' Creed underlines this. 'He was crucified, dead and buried.' Yet we affirm that he is alive.

So what happened? We don't know. Nobody saw what happened on that first Easter morning. No doubt this was due to the mercy of God. Doubtless he could have arranged for a group of onlookers to be 'in' on the resurrection. He chose not to. Perhaps no human being could have survived that burst of awesome energy.

Whatever the reason, the resurrection happened without human witnesses. So Archbishop Robert Runcie was not being evasive when he called the event itself 'a great mystery'.

- Shortly afterwards, people visited the tomb and found it empty. Jesus' body had disappeared. The first visitor thought that someone had removed it. Hence Mary Magdalene's poignant request to the gardener. 'Sir, if you have carried him away, tell me where you have put him.'

> But according to St John, Mary was not talking to a gardener. She was talking to a carpenter. It was Jesus himself, risen from the dead. This illustrates two important features of the New Testament account. First the empty tomb; then the appearances of the risen Lord. Taken together, these events convinced the first disciples that God had raised Jesus from the dead.

Their conviction was tested in the crucible. They suffered for it; some died for it. But their belief could not be shaken. This is very impressive. People will not die for their inventions. They will, and do, die for their convictions. One thing is absolutely certain. When the first disciples claimed to have seen the risen Lord, they meant what they said.

So . . . what does this long-ago, mysterious event mean for us today?

PROBING THE MEANING

The resurrection of Jesus Christ from the dead — if it happened — is clearly an amazing event. But the New Testament (which claims that it *did* happen) asserts that it is not merely a *wonderful* event. It is a *highly significant* event — for two main reasons:

1. JESUS IS ALIVE. Some Christians put all their weight on the present tense. The Bishop of Durham, for example, David Jenkins claims to believe in 'a spiritual resurrection, a transforming resurrection, a real resurrection'. The *Spirit* of Jesus is with us, so he would not worry if the bones of Jesus were to be found. For him it is the present-day significance of those Easter events which matters.

What *really* counts, argues the Bishop, is the love and power of Jesus NOW. Not what happened (or didn't happen) two thousand years ago.

All Christians agree with the first part of that argument. Jesus is alive: alive today. That is the good news which the Church is privileged to declare and Christians are called to share. We claim that Jesus is active in the modern world. Not simply through his marvellous teaching. Not only by his matchless example. But by his living Spirit. If we allow him to do so, he will inspire us, challenge us, guide us, renew us.

But many modern Christians disagree strongly with the Bishop of Durham over the importance of history. In their view, a resurrection which leaves Jesus rotting in the tomb is not really a resurrection at all.

The Bishop of Durham and his supporters sometimes give the impression that it is a matter of simple (naïve?) believers on the one hand *versus* deep thinkers on the other hand. (I'll leave you to work out which is which!) But this won't do. Many fine minds, including some of his fellow bishops, are against David Jenkins on this point. (See *Christ is Risen* by Richard Harries, Bishop of Oxford; and *Evidence for the Resurrection* by John Austin Baker, Bishop of Salisbury. Both Mowbray). Many would agree with Archbishop George Carey when he says:

> I believe that the physical resurrection is at the very heart of the Christian faith.

Perhaps a refusal to embrace the empty tomb arises from a failure of nerve, rather than from profound scholarship? Bodily resurrection is a tough belief requiring robust faith in an unbelieving world.

2. **DEATH IS DEAD.** I parked my car and opened the boot. Then I became aware of a fast car speeding down the narrow street. So I stepped back on to the pavement to let it pass. As I did so our three-year-old neighbour came from his front door, trotted along the pavement and started to cross the road. Before I could shout, there was a dull thud. I drew a deep breath and went to Billy as he lay in the road . . .

Next week I attended Billy's funeral. By then I had seen him trot, and heard that awful thud, a hundred times – in the action replay on that inner video recorder, which we call memory and imagination.

It is a harsh fact that life is given to us without guarantees. We live only once and we all live more-or-less dangerously. Terrible things happen to lovely people, and some people seem to get more – much more – personal tragedy than they deserve.

Even if we live calm, untragic lives, the only certainty is that they will end. Even more devastating: so will the lives of those whom we love and cherish. In a hundred years other feet will walk our streets. As the anti-Christian philosopher Nietzsche observed, we are 'the brotherhood of death'.

For most of us, most of the time, these awesome truths don't press very hard. We are too busy paying the gas bill, feeding the cat, going to work and enjoying our weekends, to spend long on eternal matters.

But from time to time deep questions break in and disturb. Do we really worry our way through seventy-or-so years only to be put out like a candle? Will that final illness or sudden accident really be the end of me? Or is there more? Can we look for a richer, fuller life beyond the grave? If we could – with integrity and without wishful thinking – settle that question with a resounding 'yes', then we really would feel differently about our daily lives.

So the implications of the resurrection of Jesus are immense – and practical. We are not on our own. He is with us (Matt. 28:20). We do not live in a cold, uncaring universe. Death does not have the final word (1 Cor. 15:54).

'Death is optional' claims a modern American guru. Yes, we do live longer than ever before. Yes, we can delay corruption with lead-lined coffins. But the claim itself is false. Arrogant. Absurd. Evasive. Crass. Mark Twain was much more accurate. 'No-one gets out alive'.

In the face of this terrifying fact, the Bible asserts that Jesus is 'the resurrection and the life'. In other words, while the first Easter story describes a unique and wonderful event, it is not an *isolated* event. It has enormous implications.

The resurrection of Jesus is described in the New Testament as 'the first fruits of a great harvest'. *We* are that harvest. Because God raised Jesus, he will raise us. Because Jesus defeated death, we shall inherit eternal life. To change the picture: by his resurrection Jesus flung wide open the gates of glory. We are invited and welcomed to join the vibrant life of heaven. In the light of this glorious fact, other questions press for attention.

(a) *Will I have a body?*   Most of us are happy with the idea of eternal life. But some are less happy with the actual words of the Creed: 'I believe in the resurrection of the body.' Many people prefer the notion of spiritual survival or the soul 'marching on'. The Bible is much more earthy. When it talks of the glories of heaven, the New Testament does so in terms of bodily resurrection, rather than spiritual survival. By *resurrection* the New Testament writers do not mean mere *resuscitation*. What is raised will be far more glorious than what is 'sown' – just as the butterfly is much lovelier than the caterpillar.

In groping for words to convey this great truth, the apostle Paul used the paradox, 'spiritual body'. We get a clue about the meaning of this from the Gospel records, when they describe the resurrection appearances of Jesus. On being raised he had a *real* body – a body which carried the scars of crucifixion. His disciples actually touched him; here was no ghost! His was a transformed, more glorious body. He was not readily recognised; he could appear and disappear at will; locked doors could not exclude him.

(b) *Will I still be me?*   Modern minds addressing this difficult, but fascinating and important subject, sometimes find it helpful to focus on the word 'personality'. The teaching of the Bible is that we shall retain our personalities – refined and purified – for all eternity. You will still be recognisably 'you'. We shall be much more interesting and glorious than we are now; but there will be a definite link between you-as-you-are-now, and you-as-you-will-be-then.

Every aspect of your life which you offered to God on earth, will be gloriously raised – and handed back to you. In heaven, we shall not lose our identity. Indeed, it is only then that we shall really find and possess our true selves. For the qualities which make us what we are, are on loan now. They will be *given* to us then – and they will be ours for ever.

No wonder St Paul could say that he wanted to depart and be with Christ. No wonder Malcolm Muggeridge could say that he was looking forward to death – as he would look forward to leaving a seedy hostel and booking into a magnificent hotel (with all expenses paid!).

(c) *How can I know?*   Is it a question of 'pie in the sky when you die'? When thoughts of death (my own or someone close to me) press in, I want to believe in heaven. So I must beware of wishful thinking. The Christian assertion that death is dead takes us to the heart of life's deepest mystery. Does it stand on solid ground? Is there any evidence?

Yes there is. Strong evidence. But evidence is different from conclusive proof. There is no sequence of watertight arguments which will convince every unbeliever that God raised Jesus from the dead. The world is not like that. God did not intend it to be.

But there are reasons to support this belief — strong reasons.

> It is still very important, in a sceptical and often hostile culture, that the Easter story should stand up to attack — no easy matter at a distance of almost two thousand years. But stand up it does. (*John Austin Baker, Bishop of Salisbury*.)

I have attempted to assemble some of the considerable evidence for the resurrection of Jesus elsewhere (*The Case Against Christ*; Hodder 1986. Chapters 16–17). So I won't go over much of that ground again here. But we will look at four factors which point in the direction of resurrection:

(a) The way the world is
(b) Making sense of history
(c) Making sense of experience
(d) Weighty witnesses

1. The way the world is

'I have only seen a ghost once.' That nicely understated sentence from a book by Canon Stafford Wright sticks in my mind. For ghosts, unlike elephants, are not objects which the hopeful might plan to see on safari in East Africa.

C. S. Lewis used the same device in *Miracles*. He wrote about a woman who claimed to have seen a ghost. Interestingly, she continued to disbelieve in ghosts. 'I must be mistaken,' she said. Despite the evidence presented to her senses, she was convinced that the world simply isn't like that.

'What the world is like' is a vital ingredient in our investigation. Viewed in one way, our experience comes out *against* resurrection. Scores of people die every day. They do not get up and walk.

We live in a dependable, predictable world. A world where apples fall downwards, where day follows night (unless you live in the Arctic) and where winter follows summer (unless you live on the Equator). We can predict (within limits) what will and will not happen. Science seems to confirm our commonsense view of the world as reliable and straightforward.

But not completely. For one thing, modern scientists present us with a much more mysterious universe than scientists of an earlier generation. Modern science often challenges commonsense. It paints a picture of a less-than-solid world. The table on which I am writing feels secure enough. But I am assured that it is mainly empty space, populated by zooming waves of energy.

Furthermore, science thrives on the unexpected. Scientists can never close their minds to the unpredictable. They must not decide in advance what is and is not possible. As Professor John Polkinghorne puts it, 'The scientist's instinctive reaction is not to ask the question,

"What is it reasonable to believe?", but . . . "what appears to be the case?"'

Of course, scientists must not be gullible. But it is by probing the unexpected that some new hypotheses are born and deeper understanding gained. If water boils at 90 °C instead of the usual 100°C, a scientist does not say, 'impossible'. He says, 'how interesting' – and looks for other factors. When he discovers that this lower boiling point always occurs on mountains, he considers the relationship between temperature and air pressure.

A good scientist keeps an open mind for a while at least – refusing to decide in advance what will and will not happen; what is and is not possible. His senses will be alert to surprise, for that is where breakthroughs are likely to come.

Rumours. The universe is surprising in other ways too. Our world is full of rumours. Rumours of unidentified flying objects; of spoons bent by rubbing; of near-death experiences; of people behaving oddly under hypnosis; of telepathic communications; of corn circles; of miracles; of poltergeists; of prayers that have been answered; of fakirs walking unburned on red hot coals. The list could go on . . .

No, I am not suggesting for one minute that we should believe all these things. We are wise to be cautious. I don't doubt that at least 95 per cent of such accounts and claims are false – through deliberate deceit or genuine error. But it seems less easy to dissolve away the final 5 per cent. This residue gives sober investigators pause for thought. Our world is a mixture of reliability, surprise, and mystery. As Hamlet put it: 'There are more things in heaven and earth, Horatio, than are dreamt of in your philosophy.'

But even if 100 per cent of such reports can be explained away, it remains true that we live in a world where life leads to death, and death leads to life, in the cycle of growth. The very seasons can point us towards resurrection, if we have a mind to let them do so.

> Our Lord has written the promise of resurrection, not in books alone, but in every leaf in springtime (*Martin Luther*).

None of this amounts to evidence for the resurrection of Jesus. It simply prepares some minds to receive it. Evidence lies elsewhere – in history and personal experience.

2. Making sense of history

Professor C. F. D. Moule of Cambridge reviewed some of the evidence for the resurrection and then put this question. If we find 'a great hole in history, a hole of the size and shape of resurrection, what does the secular historian propose to stop it up with?'

'A great hole in history . . . the size and shape of resurrection.' He was referring to the astonishing fact that the Church exploded with such vigour, force and transforming power in such unlikely circumstances.

Consider. Jesus died on the cross. He left no writings. His followers were shattered: depressed, demoralised and ashamed. They had no creative energy. All some of them could do was return to the family fishing business.

That was entirely understandable, for few of his male followers had emerged from the trial and execution of Jesus with honour. They had deserted, denied and betrayed him. Worse still, the authorities who crucified Jesus might well be after them too.

But suddenly they were out on the streets preaching boldly; laughing at persecution and punishment. Unafraid, joyful, confident. Their faith was contagious. Despite the dangers, their movement grew and grew and grew. The unhappenable happened. It engulfed the mighty Roman empire.

What transformed those first disciples into that dynamic, creative force? *Answer*: an unshakeable conviction that God had raised Jesus from the dead. They may have been wrong; but one thing is clear. They passionately believed it to be the case. This was no invention, for men will not die for a fraud or for a hoax.

They based their belief on three factors. *First*, the borrowed tomb in which Jesus had been laid, was empty. *Second*, the Lord had appeared to some of them after his death — not as a ghost but as a real person, scars and all. *Third*, after his ascension, even those followers who didn't visit the empty tomb or see the risen Lord, were convinced that he was with them — by his living Spirit.

Mistake? If they weren't lying — and they weren't — perhaps they were mistaken? A bad case of hallucinations maybe? On close investigation that line of argument cannot be sustained either. People can hallucinate in groups — when taking drugs for example. But each person will see a different hallucination. What people 'see' comes from deep inside the subconscious mind, and this differs from person to person just as fingerprints do.

The disciples all saw the same thing. Or rather, they all saw the same person. JESUS.

3. Making sense of experience

Countless believers testify to a common experience. They are 'accompanied' through life by an unseen Presence. They relate this settled conviction to the promise of Jesus: 'And surely I am with you always, to the very end of the age' (Matt. 28:20).

As we might expect, this experience is both comforting and *un*comfortable. From this conviction we draw strength and confidence. By this same conviction we are challenged to love, service and holiness.

As we might not expect, this experience – and the conviction arising from it – is found in people from every culture, social background and personality type. Often it is a quiet conviction, without dramatic evidence to support it. Sometimes it is focused in a remarkable way.

Archbishop Anthony Bloom provides a significant example. Surgeon; member of the wartime resistance movement; head of the Russian Orthodox Church in Britain. He is deeply impressive. Strength, sanity, stillness and serenity are words which come to mind.

As a young unbeliever he heard a lecture on Christianity which made him angry. But he knew he could not dismiss it without investigation. So he began to read St Mark's Gospel (Mark is the shortest Gospel; he did not intend to waste time on the exercise!).

In *School for Prayer* he describes what happened next:

> Before I reached the third chapter, I suddenly became aware that on the other side of my desk there was a presence. And the certainty was so strong that it was Christ standing there that it has never left me. This was the real turning point. Because Christ was alive and I had been in his presence I could say with certainty that what the Gospel said about the crucifixion of the prophet of Galilee was true, and the centurion was right when he said, 'Truly he is the Son of God.'

The fact that this experience came out of the blue to a young *un*believer makes it thought-provoking. The fact that Anthony Bloom is such a strong, stable person makes it convincing. The fact that it relates to the (often less dramatic) experience of millions of other people in every age, makes it compelling – for me at least.

4. Weighty witnesses

In a court of law, expert and surprising witnesses are sometimes called – those with special expertise in the subject under consideration, or people whose background and insights might lead the jury to expect them to come down on the other side. I want to call three such witnesses

As an expert witness I call upon a scientist who has reflected long and hard on 'the way the world is' (the title of his SPCK paperback). Referring to the remarkable confidence of the disciples following the death of Jesus, John Polkinghorne writes:

It is an astonishing transformation. Something happened to bring it about. Whatever it was it must have been of a magnitude commensurate with the effect it produced. I believe that it was the resurrection of Jesus from the dead.

Then two surprises. Both are Jewish scholars with no Christian axe to grind. Indeed, we might expect them to reject the Christian claim. Dr Geza Vermes wrote this about that first Easter morning:

First, the women belonging to the entourage of Jesus discovered an empty tomb and were definite that it was *the* tomb. Second, the rumour that the apostles stole that body is most improbable. From the psychological point of view, they would have been too depressed and shaken to be capable of such a dangerous undertaking. But above all, since neither they nor anyone else expected a resurrection, there would have been no purpose in faking one.

Professor Pinchas Lapide goes even further: 'I accept the resurrection of Jesus not as an invention of the community of disciples, but as a historical event.'

But perhaps the weightiest witnesses are those who have experienced the transforming power of the resurrection in a profound way. I have met people whose lives were in a mess – drug addicts and thieves for example. Today they are living stable, honest lives. It was not a question of turning over a new leaf, or pulling up their socks. They lacked the moral vision and spiritual strength to put their own lives in order. No. They claim to have met the risen Lord; they talk of finding a new sense of direction and a new source of energy. Such testimony is not easily discounted.

CORE QUESTIONS . . .

For Group Discussion and Individual Reflection

		Yes/No

1. (a) As a child did you suffer bereavement at the loss of a pet? ....

    (b) As a child did you suffer bereavement at the loss of someone special? ....

    (c) As an adult have you suffered bereavement? ....

    (d) Did any of the following help you to cope: ....

    – the funeral service? ....
    – the pastoral ministry of the Church? ....
    – the funeral director? ....
    – friends and/or family? ....
    – belief in the resurrection of Jesus? ....
    – belief in the resurrection of the body? ....
    – belief in heaven? ....
    – anything else? ....

    (e) Do you believe you will see that person again? ....

2. (a) Do you often think about your own death? ....

    (b) Are you afraid of death? ....

    (c) Are you afraid of dying? ....

(d) Do you believe that you will go to
heaven?   ....

(e) Do you believe that everyone will
go to heaven?   ....

(f) Do you think that awareness of
death grows with the passing
years?   ....

(g) In your experience, do many
people push death to the back of
their minds even in old age?   ....

3. Have you ever thought about your own funeral? If
not, do so now!
(a) Do you want a sombre or a joyful mood?
(b) Choose two hymns and one Bible reading.
(c) Is New Testament teaching about the resurrection of Jesus important to you as you consider
these issues?
(d) Have you made a will? You may not wish to
discuss this: you may wish to act upon it soon!

4. Would it be helpful/intrusive to use questions 1–3 as
the basis for a survey of belief among friends and
neighbours? (Partly as genuine research – we need to
understand people's views; partly as a pastoral aid –
some might be glad to talk about these deep issues;
partly as an aid to evangelism.)

5. The Bishop of Durham thinks of himself as a missionary and evangelist. He is so keen to communicate
the good news that he wants to remove unnecessary
stumbling blocks for modern people. Hence his
insistence that you can believe in 'a spiritual resurrection, a transforming resurrection, a real resurrection', without believing in the bodily resurrection of

Jesus. Is he right to 'remove' a substantial part of this miracle? Is this likely to bring more people to faith in God?

6. I have just received a letter which describes a transformation. Having 'met Christ' a shabby, under-confident man is now confident and clean.
   (a) Do you know of such transformations (see also bottom of page 115)?
   (b) Do you think they are related to the resurrection of Jesus?
   (c) Do you know of people who have 'shrunk' rather than grown on joining a church? (e.g. over-dependence; narrowing of interests)

BIBLE STUDY   Read 1 Corinthians 15:58. St Paul isn't talking to Christian ministers – but to Corinthian slaves. Their 'labour in the Lord' was not preaching but scrubbing loos and washing up. But because of the resurrection it was 'not in vain'; God would use their work in his wider purposes.

What is *your* 'daily labour'? Do you feel that you do it 'in the Lord'? Do you find St Paul's words encouraging, frustrating, hopelessly idealistic or . . .

. . . AND MORE QUESTIONS

Please read the note in chapter 1 entitled 'Why More Questions' at this point

7. Christians sometimes argue about prayers for the dead. Critics say that such prayers undermine confidence in the finished work of Christ. Why pray, if the faithful are in heaven? But the bereaved often feel

that prayer brings them 'closer' to their loved ones. What do you feel about this?

8. St Peter challenges us to be ready 'to give the reason for the hope that you have' (1 Pet. 3:15). Can you?

9. A widow is urged by friends to 'get in touch' with her husband at a spiritualist meeting. Her vicar is strongly against this and the widow asks for advice. What would you say?

10. Our world is predictable, surprising and mysterious – all at the same time.

    (a) Do you agree? Does this help as you consider the notion of resurrection?
    (b) Does the rhythm of nature – winter leading to spring; butterfly from the chrysalis – help you believe in resurrection? Or is this a sentimental distraction? (Some groups might wish to consider this in relation to the New Age Movement.)

11. What do you understand by 'the resurrection of the body' and 'eternal life'? Do you believe in them? If so, do they have any practical use?

BIBLE STUDY   Read Philippians 1:19–26. St Paul thought that heaven would be wonderful. So he said that he would rather die than live.

(a) Can you understand that viewpoint? (See Malcolm Muggeridge: Page 107.)
(b) Do you share it?
(c) If heaven is as glorious as the New Testament claims, are Christians right to oppose euthanasia?

Homework?

At the end of chapter three we used a famous devotional prayer. It stresses the approachability of Jesus: he is our friend and brother. But there is another picture of Jesus too. On the island of Patmos John was so overwhelmed by the majesty and holiness of the risen and ascended Lord that he 'fell at his feet as though dead' (Rev. 1:17). Jesus – like a gentle giant – reached out, touched John and said: 'Do not be afraid. I am the First and the Last. I am the Living One; I was dead, and behold I am alive for ever and ever! And I hold the keys of death and Hades' (Rev. 1:17–18).

Ponder these great words and perhaps compose a prayer on this theme beginning: 'Risen and Ascended Lord of Glory . . .'

VIEWPOINTS . . .

. . . On what happens after death

- KEN LIVINGSTONE MP I am an atheist, and I believe in the evolution of time, and when we die 'We are dead', to quote Bertrand Russell.

- DAVID ALTON MP Jesus' own life, death, and life beyond the grave is the confident expectation of all who love him.

- MAUREEN LIPMAN I'd like to think that we just kind of change channels . . . and have another try somewhere else . . . If there's a judgement day, I've had it.

- CHARLTON HESTON I have no idea. Obviously, like all the rest of us, I will find out.

- KINGSLEY AMIS Nothing.

- **ARCHBISHOP ROBERT RUNCIE** We are secure because in death we shall be still in the care of the One we've learnt to trust and who doesn't let us down.

. . . On resurrection

- **KALLISTOS WARE** Christ rises from the dead, and by his rising he delivers us from anxiety and terror: the victory of the cross is confirmed, love is openly shown to be stronger than hatred, and life to be stronger than death.

- **ARCHBISHOP JOHN HABGOOD** He forgave those who crucified him . . . And he demonstrated on that first Easter Day that life is stronger than death, love is more powerful than hatred, and goodness more enduring than evil. Good Friday and Easter belong together . . . together they are the guarantee of God's transforming power.

- **THOMAS ARNOLD** I know of no one fact in the history of mankind which is proved by better evidence of every sort, to the understanding of a fair enquirer, than the great sign which God has given us that Christ died and rose again from the dead.

- **ALAN RICHARDSON** Christianity is a religion of miracle, and the miracle of Christ's resurrection is the living centre and object of Christian faith.

- **JOHN STOTT** Belief in the resurrection is not an appendage to the Christian faith. It is the Christian faith.

- **PROFESSOR SIR NORMAN ANDERSON** Frankly, I myself find the evidence for the resurrection completely convincing.

- **LORD RAMSEY** It is the message of the Bible, in all its richness, that people of our generation need . . . the Bible has the resurrection as its key. Its God is the God who raised up Jesus Christ from the dead.

· **JOHN DONNE**
  Death be not proud, though some have called thee
  Mighty and dreadfull, for, thou art not soe . . .
  One short sleepe past, wee wake eternally,
  And death shall be no more, Death thou shalt die.

· **ARCHBISHOP GEORGE CAREY**   I believe that Jesus was crucified, buried and that his cold dead body was raised alive by God.

MEDITATION AND PRAYER

Read John 20:10–18. Go over the details in your mind: Mary's distress and desperation turning to joy. Keep that picture in your mind but replace Mary with yourself. Hear Jesus say *your* name. Walk together in the early morning sunshine and accept his invitation to share with him your worries, your fears, your joys. (You *can* – for prayer is precisely that. Why not do it now?)

Keep silence together

Collect for Easter 1

Almighty Father,
  who in your great mercy made glad the disciples
    with the sight of the risen Lord:
  give us such knowledge of his presence with us,
  that we may be strengthened and sustained
    by his risen life
  and serve you continually in righteousness and
    truth;
  through Jesus Christ our Lord.

He Descended . . . Ascended . . . Will Come Again to Judge

Therefore God exalted him to the highest place (Phil. 2:9).

They will see the Son of Man coming on the clouds of the sky, with power and great glory (Matt. 24:30).

GETTING STARTED

God leads a pretty sheltered life

At the end of time, billions of people were scattered on a vast plain before God's throne. Some groups talked heatedly. 'How can God judge us? What does he know about suffering?', snapped a young woman. She jerked back a sleeve to reveal a tattooed number from a Nazi concentration camp. A black man lowered his collar. 'What about this?' he demanded, showing an ugly rope burn. 'Lynched for no crime but being black. We have suffocated in slave ships, been wrenched from loved ones, toiled till only death gave release.'

Many others recounted stories of suffering. Each had a complaint against God for the evil and suffering he permitted in his world. How lucky he was to live in heaven where all was sweetness and light; where there was no weeping, no fear, no hunger, no hatred. All agreed that God leads a pretty sheltered life.

So each group sent out a representative. There was a

Jew, a black woman, an untouchable from India, an illegitimate child, a victim from Hiroshima, a sweatshop worker, a prisoner from a labour camp. In the centre of the plain they consulted.

At last they were ready to present their case. It was very daring. Before God could qualify to be their judge, he must endure what they had endured. So the decision was made: God should be sentenced to live on earth – as a man! But, because he was God, they set certain safeguards to be sure he could not use his divine powers to help himself:

Let him be born a Jew.

Let the legitimacy of his birth be doubted, so that none will know who is really his father.

Let him champion a cause so just, but so radical, that it brings down upon him the hatred and condemnation of the establishment.

Let him try to describe what no man has ever seen, tasted, heard or smelled . . . let him try to communicate God to men.

Let him be betrayed by his dearest friends.

Let him be indicted on false charges, tried before a prejudiced jury, and convicted by a cowardly judge.

Let him be terribly alone and abandoned.

Let him be tortured.

Then let him die a humiliating death alongside common criminals.

As each leader announced a portion of the sentence, there were shouts of approval from the people. But after the final statement, there was a long silence. No one uttered another word. No one moved.

For suddenly all knew . . . God had already served his sentence.
(*The Long Silence* [amended]. Author unknown.)

SETTING IT OUT

He descended to the dead . . . He ascended into heaven, and is seated at the right hand of the Father. He will come again to judge the living and the dead.

Taken together, these statements from the Apostles' Creed carry a sackful of truths:

· Jesus shared our humanity in every detail – including death.

· Jesus transformed and glorified human nature – by taking it into heaven.

· History will not go on endlessly. God has a purpose for our world: a purpose which will come to a climax.

· Jesus will return – not as a babe in a manger but in immense, awesome splendour.

· Jesus is Judge as well as Saviour.

PROBING THE MEANING

In this section we look at eight topics which raise questions about Heaven, Hell, Judgement and Forgiveness.

1. JESUS AND HELL. At this point in the Creed, the 1662 Book of Common Prayer says, 'He descended into hell.' The word 'hell' has two meanings. First, it refers to the awful possibility of eternal separation from God. Second, it describes a 'waiting room' – a place or state where those who have died await the final judgement. The

righteous await their redemption; the unrighteous await the verdict on their lives – and on their attitude towards God and neighbour.

Jesus 'descended into hell' in *both* senses. To probe the first we can helpfully consider St Paul. As Saul of Tarsus he was convinced that Jesus was *not* the Messiah. Saul was certain about this, because he knew his Bible.

The Book of Deuteronomy clearly teaches that any man who 'is hung upon a tree' is under God's curse (Deut. 21:23). Saul knew that Jesus had been crucified upon a tree . . . Therefore Jesus was under God's curse . . . Therefore he could not possibly be God's anointed Messiah.

QED. The case was proved beyond doubt.

> The pious Jew had an especial horror of crucifixion. Because of a Mosaic curse upon a man hung upon a tree, it appeared to him as a particular sign of divine rejection . . . a crucified Messiah was an impossibility, the thought a bitter black jest. (*John Polkinghorne*.)

Following his Damascus road experience, the apostle Paul came to see that Bible verse for what it is. Not as a problem pointing *away* from Jesus as Messiah, but as a solution pointing *towards* Jesus as Saviour and Lord (Gal. 3:13).

On the cross, Jesus was indeed under a curse – for he bore the curse of human sin. In St Paul's daring phrase, 'God made him who had no sin to be sin for us' (2 Cor. 5:21). Hence his anguished cry, 'My God, my God, why have you forsaken me?' Jesus suffered as no one else has ever suffered – for he is 'the Lamb of God, who takes away the sin of the world' (John 1:29).

To put it starkly, God the Son experienced separation from God the Father. Our sins sent him to hell. Words fail us as we tremble before this terrible – yet glorious – mystery.

But Jesus went to hell in another sense too – and it is to this that the Apostles' Creed directly refers. He is 'the *man* Christ Jesus' (1 Tim. 2:5). He shared our human experience in every detail – including death. Having died, 'he descended to the dead'. Three Bible passages teach about this (Eph. 4:9; 1 Pet. 3:18–22 and 4:6). They are not easy to understand, so don't get stuck here!

The main point is that Jesus understands and supports us at every point in our lives – and especially as we go through 'the valley of the shadow of death' (Psalm 23:4). He understands because he has been there before us: 'he suffered death, so that by the grace of God he might taste death for everyone' (Heb. 2:9).

2. JESUS AND HEAVEN. Where is Jesus now? The glorious answer is – EVERYWHERE! The Holy Spirit is the Spirit of Jesus (Acts 16:7). It was because he longed to be with *all* of his people, *all* of the time, that he told his first disciples, 'it is for your good that I am going away' (John 16.7). Pentecost could not come without Calvary, followed by resurrection and ascension.

But there is another answer to the question, where is Jesus now? He is *in heaven*. The Bible tells us that he is reigning; ruling; sitting at the right hand of his Father; praying for you and me; receiving the praises of that great company of worshippers in heaven, with whom we link our earthly hymns.

'Jesus is Lord.' That earliest Christian Creed points us to the central meaning of the ascension. Having *descended* (not only to earth, but to the place of the dead), Jesus also *ascended*. Having experienced the deepest possible humiliation – pinioned naked and helpless to a cross – he was exalted by God to his rightful place as King of Kings and Lord of Lords.

This glorious truth is expressed with majestic, poetic power in the letter to the Philippians. Paul quotes an early Christian hymn (2:6–11). That hymn charts Jesus' steps downwards from the glory of heaven to the degradation of Calvary. He died there in loving obedience to the Father's will. He poured out his life as a loving sacrifice for his Father's children.

Because of Jesus' total obedience and perfect love, God has 'highly exalted him'. So he sits at God's right hand. But there is a further great truth here – a truth emphasised within the Eastern Churches. On ascending into heaven, Jesus did not shed his humanity. *He took it with him.* It is not *an angel* who sits at the Father's right hand: it is *a human being.* As the little brothers and sisters of Jesus, we share in that great honour. In him and through him, human nature has been eternally dignified, exalted, transformed and perfected.

3. JESUS AND JUDGEMENT. Some Bible teaching is unfashionable among modern Christians. In Jim Wallis' phrase, we are in danger of reading 'a Bible with holes in'. But like it or not, judgement is a central Bible theme. At the end of time the Son of Man will return – not only as Saviour but as Judge. In the words of the Creed, 'He will come again to judge the living and the dead.'

'Salvation' is a wide word. It refers to being made

whole in Christ – a process in which all creation will be caught up. But one aspect of salvation is narrow and precise. It means 'escape'.

The Bible is clear. Each of us deserves the judgement of God. 'All have sinned and fall short of the glory of God' (Rom. 3:23). But there is worse to come. If the verdict is clear and universal, so is the penalty. 'The wages of sin is death,' (Rom. 6:23).

All have sinned. *All* are guilty.

How, then, can we escape judgement? Who can be saved? The New Testament comes at this vital question from two angles.

(a) First, *justification by faith*. (See Page 56.) We human beings are the company of sinners. No one deserves salvation; no one can earn it. But we can receive it – as a gift of grace from God's open hand. We receive his offer of forgiveness *by faith*. We simply say, 'Yes please, God' and 'Thank you, Lord'. Then we are safe. Viewed from this standpoint, the Church is quite simply the company of the grateful. *Eucharist* means thanksgiving. We gather week by week to say a heartfelt thank you.

St Paul expresses the reason for our gratitude boldly and simply: 'There is now no condemnation for those who are in Christ Jesus' (Rom. 8:1).

Recently I received a phone call from a young Christian who was worried. He knows that he is a sinner; he knows too that many Bible passages speak about God's judgement. Surely this includes him?

I found myself saying something like this. The Bible – especially the Old Testament – describes God as 'long-suffering'. When the book of your life is opened, you will expect to find all those nasty, spiteful and selfish things which you did, said and thought recorded there in black and white. Even worse perhaps, you expect to find written there all the good things which you failed to do, because of indifference or pride or hostility.

> To your amazement and joy, the book will contain page after page of blank, white paper. Not because you did nothing wrong – but because your sins have been forgiven. God really does 'forgive and forget'. Because of his love for you, and all that Jesus did for you, your sins will be blotted out. 'Though your sins are like scarlet, they shall be as white as snow; though they are red as crimson, they shall be like wool' (Isa. 1:18. See also 1 John 1:8–9).

This great truth can be illustrated by a homely story. A man lost his temper. 'Please forgive me, Lord' he prayed. The following day he lost his temper again. 'Oh Lord, I've done it again,' he wailed in anguish when he cooled down. At that point a voice from heaven asked, 'Done what again?'

If this sounds too good to be true, we are in distinguished company. St Luke tells us that some of the first disciples 'disbelieved for joy' (24:41). The news of Jesus' resurrection was simply too wonderful for them to take in. The same is true for us when we consider this amazing gospel of grace. Surely it can't be *that* simple. But it is.

Well, almost . . .

(b) That's where the second angle comes in. Salvation is a gift. But like all precious gifts it needs to be received and responded to. We *receive* God's wonderful gift of salvation by faith. We *respond* with gratitude. Gratitude = action. Hence that tough story of judgement known as the Parable of the Sheep and the Goats, to which we turn shortly.

4. JUDGEMENT AND LOVE. God is not an ogre who enjoys punishing us. Quite the reverse; he loves the world which he made. Indeed, he loves the world so much that 'he gave his one and only Son, that whoever believes in him shall not perish but have eternal life' (John 3.16). The New Testament makes it clear that God's deepest desire is that *every single person* should escape hell and enter heaven (1 Tim. 2:3–5 and 2 Pet. 3:9).

But if we refuse the light which he gives; if we continue to insist on doing our own thing in our own way; then . . . so be it.

This was clearly and grimly put by a preacher who suggested that on Judgement Day only four words will be spoken. Those who respond to God will say to him: 'Your will be done.' To those who refuse to accept his way of love, God will say the same words: 'Your will be done.' Spoken by him, they assume an awful finality.

All sin tends to be addictive, and the terminal point of addiction is damnation. Since God has given us the freedom either to accept his love and obey the laws of our created nature, or to reject it and defy them, he cannot prevent us from going to hell and staying there if that is what we insist upon. (*W. H. Auden.*)

5. HEAVEN: FOR VOLUNTEERS ONLY. We can have no very exact idea as to who will be in heaven. No doubt there will be surprises, for some very wicked people may have repented at the very end – like the thief on the cross.

One thing is clear: unless we repent we shall dislike heaven intensely. For heaven means focusing our attention on Jesus, and forgetting ourselves. In heaven, love will reign supreme; hatred and indifference will be banished. Unless we are drastically changed, heaven will feel like hell: for the vibrancy, purity, holiness and joy of heaven will be totally overwhelming.

To fit us for heaven we must be changed. This will happen 'in a flash, in the twinkling of an eye' (1 Cor. 15:52). But that change must be voluntary. God will do the transforming – but only with our permission. It is rather like signing a hospital consent form for an operation. To do so involves surgery – and life. If we withhold consent, we avoid the surgery but we get steadily worse. We must give – or withhold – that permission . . . NOW. The choice is ours. Who will be our king: Jesus or ourselves?

6. PERSONAL EXPERIENCE OF HELL. I believe in hell, mainly because Jesus taught about its reality. But I have another reason, too. I have personal experience of hell. Melodramatic? No!

When I look deeply into my own life and examine my own motives and responses, I am alarmed at what I find. Some generosity of spirit and concern for others, yes. I thank God for these, for I know that they come from him. But I find other, ugly things lurking there too: jealousy, greed, self-centredness, lust, deviousness, lack of self-control . . .

I am aware that if I live on into eternity, and if the negative qualities which mark my life are left unchecked, then I shall become a nightmare. If they are fed and developed, they will consume and take me over completely. Which is another way of talking about hell. It all adds up to this: *I need a Saviour*.

For the first time I examined myself with a seriously practical purpose. And there I found what appalled me; a zoo of lusts, a bedlam of ambitions, a nursery of fears, a harem of fondled hatreds. My name was legion. (C. S. Lewis).

'What a wretched man I am! Who will rescue me from this body of death? Thanks be to God – through Jesus Christ our Lord!' (Rom. 7:24–25).

---

7. **WHERE DO I GO WHEN I DIE?** A thoughtful Christian recently put this worried question: 'Where shall I be between death and Judgement Day?' He was convinced that he would eventually go to heaven – not because he was good, but because Jesus has thrown wide open the gates of glory.

But the Bible teaches that 'the sheep' will be received into heaven on the Day of Judgement. Does this mean that we shall be stored in a 'heavenly refrigerator' for perhaps thousands of years? A fair question: to be answered with a resounding 'No!'

The problem arises because we are dealing with time and eternity. Like oil and water, they won't mix. The Bible refers to death as 'sleep'. As far as our experience is concerned, we shall find ourselves instantly in the presence of the Lord – starting the life of heaven. For when we die we pass from time to eternity, where everything is NOW. So Jesus could say to the dying thief, 'Today you will be with me in paradise' (Luke 23:43).

8. **JUSTICE IS LOVE ON A GRAND SCALE.** The Parable of the

Sheep and the Goats (Matt. 25:31—46) depicts the great day of judgement. Five points stand out;

(a) Faith in Jesus can be nominal. Those who are condemned by him, claim allegiance to him. Faith without works is dead. Our actions (or lack of them) have serious implications.

(b) Love has two opposites. The goats are condemned for their apathy and indifference, not for hatred or hostility.

(c) Jesus identifies himself with the poor and naked. To love *them* is to love *him* – which is why the righteous are surprised when the Lord praises them.

(d) Christianity refuses to be a purely spiritual religion. *This* world matters as well as the next. God is concerned with empty stomachs as well as saved souls.

(e) When addressing the great questions of heaven and hell, the New Testament focuses sharply on individual choice and responsibility towards other individuals. But love and justice might impel us to act *together* for the common good. Consider this 'parable'!

Once upon a time there was a dangerous road leading to a village. From time to time cars drove over the cliff and the people in the village organised a swift, efficient ambulance service.

One day a visitor suggested that in the long term they might save money and lives by re-routing the road. However, this meant the compulsory purchase of prime land and a great row took place.

Love is not always expressed on a person-to-person

basis. It can mean working together to change society – and that is what we call 'politics'. Some would argue that the ambulance story relates to the Parable of the Sheep and the Goats. In their view the Church consents too readily to the 'ambulance' solution (charity) rather than the 'new road' solution (political action).

They believe the Church should be a thorn in the side of the Government – lobbying *against* Third World debt, *for* just trading arrangements, *for* those sleeping in cardboard boxes, *for* the rights of unborn children, *for* a healthy environment . . . Others disagree – arguing that Jesus' parable refers to personal charity and concern.

Once upon a time, a very large ship was launched. On boarding, each person was allocated a cabin at random. When the lunch bell sounded, those with cabins near the dining room ate well – but the food ran out while others were queuing. This happened day after day and some diners felt guilty; so they gave food to those in the queue. At first, those who received scraps were delighted. But after some weeks they protested: 'Charity is good', they said, 'but what we *really* want is justice.' The ship was called HMS *The World*.

CORE QUESTIONS . . .

For Group Discussion and Individual Reflection

1. (a) A child is killed on a busy road after school. Would you sign a petition for a 'lollipop' crossing?   Yes/No
   (b) A sex-shop is planned in a street near your Church. Would you object?   Yes/No
       If so, how? ....

(c) A toxic waste dump is proposed near your home. What action, if any, would you take? ....

....

(d) The Government intends to reduce third-world aid. Would you protest?   Yes/No
If so, how? ....

2. Can you sum up your response to the Parable of the Sheep and the Goats? Surprise . . . unease . . . challenge . . . inspiration . . . terror?

3. Read the following statements and underline one to which you want to say 'Alleluia!' – or 'Shame'! Why?

- 'Keep politics out of religion'

- 'When I give food to the poor they call me a saint. When I ask why the poor have no food, they call me a communist' (Archbishop Helder Camara).

- 'I find myself, unlike the contemporary Church, thinking more and more about the next world and less and less about the third world' (Alexander Dru).

- 'The Church is not there to preserve itself' (Roy Stevens).

- 'The Christian Church is the one organisation that exists purely for the benefit of non-members' (William Temple).

- 'I am puzzled about which Bible people are reading, when they suggest religion and politics don't mix' (Archbishop Desmond Tutu).

- 'The question to be asked is not what we should give to the poor, but when will we stop taking from the poor?' (Jim Wallis).

- 'The Holy Spirit is given to be our helper, to encourage us to meet those needs which exist on our own doorstep' (Clive Calver).

4. (a) Have you ever taken political action over an issue? e.g. written to your MP; signed a petition; joined a march; chained yourself to railings . . . ? If so: *why*? If not: *why not*?

   (b) Do you think the ambulance parable makes a valid point? Should Christians sometimes unite in political action?

   (c) Must Christians always keep the law — or does conscience sometimes urge us to protest unlawfully?

   (d) Some British Christians are happy that the Church should confront the State in South Africa, Eastern Europe or Nazi Germany, but unhappy when it does so at home. Does our different situation make this reasonable — or do we have double standards?

   (e) What practical implications might all this have for you now — as an individual, as a discussion group, as a Church?

5. Please fill in quickly, but don't discuss at this point. Use as a resource as you go on. (This links with Week 5; don't spend more than 5 minutes on it.)

Do you believe in heaven? .... Yes/No/Unsure
Do you sometimes look forward to heaven? Yes/No/Unsure
Do you believe in hell? .... Yes/No/Unsure
Hell is literally fire, worms and darkness Yes/No/Unsure
Hell is separation from God .... Yes/No/Unsure

6. The Church in previous ages is often parodied for placing too much emphasis on hell and damnation. The modern Church is sometimes criticised for placing *too little* emphasis upon God's judgement and wrath:

   (a) Do you think this criticism is valid?
   (b) When did you last hear a sermon on heaven?
   (c) When did you last hear a sermon on hell?

7. I received a phone call from a distressed Christian whose uncle had died. 'He was a lovely man but he was not a believer. Is he in heaven or hell?'

   (a) Do you expect to find only Christians in heaven? What about those of other faiths, and kind atheists?
   (b) Is there such a thing as 'hidden faith' i.e. is it possible to be a disciple of Jesus without realising it?
   (c) Are we wrong to speculate about such matters?

See Page 74 for Archbishop Carey's view. I have attempted to grapple with some of these issues in *Our God is Still Too Small* (Hodder 1988).

BIBLE STUDY   When teaching about his second coming in great glory, Jesus told his disciples: 'Be on guard! Be alert!' (Mark 13:33). When pondering the same theme, Paul urged his readers to 'wake up!' (Rom. 13:11; Eph. 5:14; 1 Thess. 5:6). What might these sharp phrases mean for us in practical terms?

. . . AND MORE QUESTIONS

Please read the note in chapter 1 entitled *Why More Questions* at this point.

8. Some Christians say they are quite certain that they will go to heaven. Other people feel that this is boastful and presumptuous, smug and glib. What do you feel about this? You might find it helpful to read verses three and four of 'There is a green hill'.

9. While I must live as though I am entirely responsible for my own eternal destiny, might I hope that my faith will in some sense 'cover' my immediate family? (1 Cor. 7:12–16) Is this helpful and comforting or merely evasive – a means of avoiding evangelism within the family?

10. (a) Some Christians are 'universalists'. They believe that God's love will ultimately triumph one hundred per cent. In their view, every single human being will end up in heaven, whatever their beliefs or behaviour on earth. What do you think?

    (b) To achieve this some people believe that God will put us through a purifying process after death – the doctrine of purgatory. Others strongly disagree. They feel this blunts the urgency of choice, waters down the saving work of Christ and denies the power of God to change us 'in a flash' (1 Cor. 15:52). Views please.

11. (a) How do you envisage heaven and hell? How do your pictures relate to those in the Bible, e.g. crowns, palms, and harps . . . fire and worms, separation, darkness . . . ?

    (b) Do you share the modern worry that heaven will be dull? How could you counter this anxiety? (See *Meditation* by G. R. Evans. Page 142.)

12. Read the extract from C. S. Lewis in *Viewpoints*

(page 142). For him, Bible teaching about heaven and hell held enormous power, and had immense practical implications for the way we view our own (brief) lives and the way we view other people.

(a) Do you *really* see people as infinite beings of infinite significance – destined for heaven or hell?

(b) Do you see the world like that? If not, could it be that your outlook owes more to the Spirit of the Age than to the teaching of the Scriptures?

13. In your view does political action have:

(a) a central role
(b) a marginal role
(c) an occasional role (depending on the situation)
(d) no role
in the Christian faith?

BIBLE STUDY   Read 1 Peter 4:17 and 1 Corinthians 3:10–17 (and possibly 1 Corinthians 6:1–11 and Hebrews 10:25–27). Warning: difficult passages!

Should preaching about judgement be reserved for evangelistic meetings or stressed mainly when believers are gathered together?

Read Romans 8:1 for encouragement!

VIEWPOINTS

· In JEAN-PAUL SARTRE's play *No Exit*, three people find themselves sharing one room for all eternity. They have been carefully selected to rub one another up the wrong way:

'So this is hell, I'd never have believed it. You remember we were all told about the torture chambers, the fire and brimstone, the burning marl. Old wives' tales. There's no need for red-hot pokers. Hell is . . . other people.'

T. S. ELIOT disagreed with the French playwright and in *The Cocktail Party* he used the line, 'Hell is oneself.' (You might care to consider whether the French or the Anglo-American playwright is more accurate.)

G. R. EVANS . . . Hell is a failure of that live, bright communication with other people and with God which is the high experience of heaven. If heaven is living in sharp focus, hell is existence in dull mutual misunderstanding.

ROGER STOTT It is possible for us to build our own hell: an impregnable castle which shuts out all possibility of relationship, a dark feeding upon oneself which is impervious to the grace that either God or man could bring.

PROFESSOR ROWAN WILLIAMS Hell stands for . . . those appallingly destructive things within us which are just there and which we have to look at, even contemplate, look full in the face, before we can grow as human beings at all.

JOHN BUNYAN The men then asked, What must we do in the Holy Place? To whom it was answered, You must receive the Comfort of all your Toil, and have Joy for all your Sorrow . . . There your eyes shall be delighted with seeing, and your ears with hearing the pleasant Voice of the *Mighty One*. There you shall enjoy your Friends again, that are gone thither before you.

JOHN CALVIN commenting on the phrase 'seated at the right hand of God the Father'. This is 'a similitude borrowed from princes . . . the subject here considered is not the posture of His body, but the majesty of His empire.'

· C. S. LEWIS   It may be possible for each to think too much of his own potential glory hereafter; it is hardly possible for him to think too often or too deeply about that of his neighbour . . . The dullest and most un-interesting person you talk to may one day be a creature which, if you saw it now, you would be strongly tempted to worship, or else a horror and a corruption which you now meet, if at all, only in a nightmare. All day long we are, in some degree, helping each other to one or other of these destinations. It is in the light of these overwhelming possibilities . . . that we should conduct all our dealings with one another, all friend-ships, all loves, all play, all politics. There are no ordinary people.

MEDITATION AND PRAYER

First reader:

· And God himself will be with them and be their God. He will wipe every tear from their eyes. There will be no more death or mourning or crying or pain. (Rev. 21:3–4).

Second reader:

· G. R. EVANS   To modern eyes it (heaven) seems beauti-ful but dull. This conception of sameness as tedious is a relatively modern one. It depends on our idea of time. Boredom requires longish stretches of time to take hold. We should not think of heaven as being in one place for endless 'time'. We should be envisaging a freedom from the confinement of time and space which will make it possible for us to be with all our friends at once and individually, to be enjoying an infinite variety of things as we choose, without delay or hurry, crowding or isolation. It is something new, a new quality of life.

Third reader:

· 'Be ready,' said the Saviour to his disciples, 'for the Son of man is coming at an hour you do not expect' (Matt. 24:44). How does one get and stay ready? By keeping short accounts with God and men; by taking life a day at a time, as Jesus told us to do (Matt. 6:34) and by heeding the advice of Bishop Ken's hymn, 'Live each day as if thy last.' Budget and plan for an ordinary span of years, but in spirit be packed up and ready to leave at any time. This should be part of our daily devotional discipline (Dr J. I. Packer).

Now keep silence   Read 1 John 3:2–3

Collect for Pentecost 21:

Eternal Father,
whose Son Jesus Christ ascended to the throne of
  heaven
that he might rule over all things as Lord:
keep the Church in the unity of the Spirit
and in the bond of his peace,
and bring the whole created order to worship at his
  feet;
who is alive and reigns with you and the Holy Spirit,
one God, now and for ever.

WEEK 7

I BELIEVE . . . IN THE HOLY SPIRIT

Jesus, full of the Holy Spirit, returned from the Jordan and was led by the Spirit in the desert (Luke 4:1).

The Spirit helps us in our weakness . . . the Spirit himself intercedes for us (Rom. 8:26).

GETTING STARTED

The Spirit . . . was a *fact of experience* in the lives of the earliest Christians. (Professor James Dunn)

* * *

Doris Brown was a remarkable woman. Six and a half feet tall, her physical presence was matched by her personality. BIG. An infectious laugh and an infectious faith. Doris was called by God to work as a missionary in China under the umbrella of SPG (now USPG: the United Society for the Propagation of the Gospel).

She was working in China in the late 1940s when the Communists took control. They would not tolerate people who viewed life from a different standpoint, so they set to work on Doris. Brainwashing began: endless hours of questioning. Doris became confused, but in the middle of her confusion she remembered a remarkable promise of Jesus concerning the Holy Spirit:

But when they arrest you, do not worry about what to

say or how to say it. At that time you will be given what to say, for it will not be you speaking, but the Spirit of your Father speaking through you (Matt. 10: 19–20).

This is not a promise that many British Christians need very often (thank God). It certainly isn't an escape clause for those with sermons to preach or talks to give. Our calling is to work hard at preparation. The setting for the promise is clear: persecution. Doris was in that setting, so she asked God for the words to say.

In response to her prayer, the Holy Spirit 'gave' to Doris the Apostles' Creed – those ancient (yet modern) statements of belief which we are studying. To each question from her persecutors she made a statement of faith, working through the Creed clause by clause:

I believe in God the Father Almighty.
I believe in Jesus Christ his only Son our Lord.
I believe in the Holy Ghost.
I believe in . . .

. . . then back to the beginning again.

Eventually her interrogators gave up. Later, Doris returned to England – with her faith intact.

SETTING IT OUT

The Holy Spirit in the Old Testament

When I first studied the Bible, it seemed to me that a rather fierce God the Father dominated the Old Testament. As far as I was concerned, the other two Persons of the Trinity arrived in the New Testament as a kind of Christian postscript.

I was wrong!

Jesus was the Father's agent in creation (Col. 1:16). And in the second verse in the Bible we read that the Spirit of God was present when God created the world. '. . . and the Spirit of God was hovering over the waters' (Gen. 1:2).

Throughout the Old Testament, God's Spirit was active — although his explicit activity was fairly limited. He inspired key individuals with special gifts for special tasks — craftsmen and musicians for example (Exod. 31:3; 35:31). And the Spirit inspired prophets to speak in the name of the Lord (Num. 24:2; Ezek. 11:5).

The Holy Spirit in the New Testament

In the Gospels we read quite a lot about God's Spirit. John the Baptist looked forward to the time when Jesus would baptise with the Holy Spirit. The Spirit anointed Jesus at his baptism. Jesus taught about the Holy Spirit, and when he set out his manifesto for ministry, he did so in the power of the Spirit (Luke 4:14, 18).

But the real watershed occurs at the beginning of the Acts of the Apostles. On the day of Pentecost, the Spirit came upon 120 believers. They 'were filled with the Holy Spirit' (Acts 2:4). This was seen as fulfilment of a promise of Jesus and a prophecy of Joel (Acts 1:8; 2:16). Centuries before, the prophet Joel had looked forward to the day when God's Spirit would not be selective. He would come in full power upon each and every one of God's people. Peter announced the glorious truth. That day has arrived; a new age has dawned.

During his lifetime on earth, Christ's presence could be experienced only by a small group of men at any given time. Now Christ dwells through the Spirit in the hearts of all those who have received him as Saviour. (*Billy Graham*).

PROBING THE MEANING

What follows? LOTS . . .

What a difference the Spirit makes! We will consider eleven aspects.

1. **THE SPIRIT BRINGS UNITY.** The New Testament is very hot on this; it is one of the great truths about Whitsun. That first Christian Pentecost was Babel in reverse. In Genesis 11 we read a deeply significant story. Human pride brought God's judgement, when men built the fabulous tower at Babel. The result was disruption and an inability to communicate. Communities were divided.

In contrast, on the day of Pentecost we find people from different countries, with different languages, hearing and understanding the same message.

This was God's way of declaring that his mercy is for *all*. By means of the Good News he would reconcile his divided family (Eph. 2:13–22). *In Christ, the curse of Babel gives way to the blessing of Pentecost.* Division and conflict are (or should be) replaced by unity and harmony. The title of one of David Watson's influential books captures this great emphasis: *One in the Spirit*.

2. **THE SPIRIT BRINGS GOD NEAR.** The Bible speaks about the greatness of God. He is transcendent; enthroned in heaven.

It speaks too about the closeness, or 'immanence', of God. God comes near in his Son and by his Spirit. The Son and the Spirit are closely related. Jesus told his disciples that it was good for them that he should go away – for he would send the Counsellor (John 16:7, 13). He was referring to his Spirit; the Holy Spirit. ·

Unlike God's Son while he walked the earth, God's Spirit would be with every disciple at every moment. Clearly this relates to some of the wonderful promises made by Jesus. Promises like: '. . . where two or three come together in my name, there am I with them.' (Matt. 18:20). And surely I am with you always, to the very end of the age' (Matt. 28:20).

He is with us, *by his Spirit* – bringing strength, power and inspiration. This great truth is summed up in the title of a book by Bishop John V. Taylor. The Holy Spirit is the *Go-Between God*. So Christian faith involves experience of the God who is with us – closer than breathing. God's Spirit warms us up. Our faith involves both duty and joy.

> How can you have a vital relationship with the living Lord Jesus without some experience? . . . Certainly we must beware of seeking experiences just for their own sake . . . But the New Testament Christian should know a quality of love and joy, life and peace that the world can neither give nor take away . . . (*David Watson*.)

In the New Testament, the Holy Spirit is described as the Counsellor, the Spirit of God, the Spirit of Christ, the Spirit of Jesus, the Spirit of the Lord, the Spirit of Truth, the Spirit . . . At first sight this appears confusing. In fact it reflects the richness of Christian experience. The early

Christians knew that God the Father and Jesus his Son were enthroned in heaven. They also knew that they were with them in their daily worries and joys. So they stretched language to its limits to describe their new experience and to explain their enlarged understanding of God.

3. THE SPIRIT BRINGS NEW LIFE. In his letter to the Colossians, St Paul speaks about God's 'secret' or 'mystery'. It is an open secret: available to all who will listen. God's secret, God's mystery, is this: 'Christ in you, the hope of glory' (Col. 1:27).

The moral teaching of Jesus is matchless. The glorious example of Jesus is inspiring. But if these form the heart and centre of the Christian faith, we do not have 'good news'; we have hard law. For Jesus' teaching and example set standards which are way beyond us. I need more – much more – than moral direction. I need inspiration, fellowship, strength and forgiveness. I need good news – not just good advice and fine example.

This is illustrated by Oscar Peterson, the great jazz pianist. As a boy he was good – very good – and big-headed too. His father knew that scolding Oscar wouldn't help. Instead he bought him a record of Art Tatum – probably the greatest piano virtuoso that jazz has ever known.

Young Oscar was inspired by the playing on the record. But he was also depressed. It was too good; it set an unattainable standard. So he gave up playing and had crying fits at night!

Now when I read the moral teaching of Jesus, and when I ponder the matchless example of Jesus, I feel like Oscar Peterson. Inspired – then depressed. For this is

Division One. And I am in Division Four. But my depression doesn't last. For important as the teaching and example of Jesus are, they are not the heartbeat of the Christian life. No. At its centre we find a *relationship*.

Christ in us, by his Spirit.

Indeed, without this relationship there is no authentic Christian faith. St Paul puts this bluntly: 'if anyone does not have the Spirit of Christ, he does belong to Christ' (Rom. 8:9).

> Being a Christian means . . . being people in whom his (Jesus') life and character and power are manifest and energised . . . Christian experience is not so much a matter of imitating a leader . . . as accepting and receiving a new quality of life – a life infinitely more profound and dynamic and meaningful than human life without Christ (*Harry Williams*).

4. THE SPIRIT PRODUCES FRUIT. There is a great deal in the New Testament about growth and progress. As a pilgrim people we are – or should be – on the move. We cannot stand still; either we are moving or we are stagnating. Various word pictures point in this direction.

For example, St Paul talks about the 'fruit of the Spirit'. God wants to grow a lovely harvest within our lives. He names nine different qualities: love, joy, peace, patience, kindness, goodness, faithfulness, gentleness and self-control (Gal. 5:22–23). All Christians are called to be open to God's activity in their lives – so every one of these qualities should become apparent in every believer.

To see a person become more loving, more open, more

generous, more tranquil, more aware of the needs of others, is a joyful experience. It is living proof of the reality of the Holy Spirit.

5. THE SPIRIT BRINGS GIFTS. The *gifts* of the Spirit are different from the *fruit* of the Spirit. One big difference is this: while every Christian is called to cultivate every one of the nine qualities listed above, no single Christian has all the gifts. That is God's way of working. He equips his church for worship, witness and loving service by scattering his gifts around. Quite literally in the Greek, he 'dollops out' his gifts among his people. Some seem to have lots; others, very few. But every single Christian has at least one gift (Matt. 25:15; 1 Cor. 12:7; 1 Pet. 4:10).

Some Christians use the more striking gifts (like speaking in tongues or healing) as the litmus test of Christian life and growth. Because God gives different gifts to different members, this is (in my view) a big mistake. Some Christian leaders have never received these particular gifts. Are we to say that they are blocking God's activity in their lives?

But we should not shelter behind this. We are called to 'eagerly desire' God's gifts in our lives (1 Cor. 12:31; 14:1). So we need to open ourselves to the possibility that God wants to give us more and more. Let's be ambitious!

These gifts are given to us by God 'for the common good' (1 Cor. 12:7). My gifts are not 'mine' for personal use and advantage. They are to be shared and used within the body of Christ – and they equip us to serve our troubled and divided world.

6. THE SPIRIT BRINGS HEALING. *(Note: Personally, I have more reason to thank God for the ministry of hospitality, generosity and administration, than for the ministry of*

healing. I select this gift for special comment, not because I think it more important – but because it is topical, controversial, important and intrinsically interesting.)

A group was walking by the sea when one member twisted her knee on a steep path. It looked serious. She was in great pain and couldn't move; they began to think of the emergency services. Her husband was at the back of the straggling group and he hurried to her. She hit him in annoyance! 'If you'd been with me, this wouldn't have happened.' He laid his hands on her knee and prayed. Quickly she was better and continued the rough walk.

On two other occasions that same man (a friend; I know he is honest) has been involved in healings so remarkable that they have startled the doctors. One was a broken bone; the other was skin cancer.

This looks like a commentary on the words of the Oxford scholar Austin Farrer: 'The miracles of the saints never cease: a hundred years ago the sainted Curé d'Ars multiplied bread and healed the sick and lived himself by a continuous physical miracle, nor has he lacked successors since.'

None of this should surprise us. We believe in the living God and we know that Jesus is alive. He is the same 'yesterday and today and for ever' (Heb. 13:8). About twenty gifts of the Spirit are listed in the New Testament and these include 'gifts of healing' and 'miraculous powers' (1 Cor. 12:9–10). But we need to note three further points:

(a) Healing is not automatic. My friend has a ministry of healing but he doesn't pretend that it always 'works'. He is no magician. Some faithful members of his Church have been seriously ill for a long time – and they remain unhealed. It seems that they are called by God (for the present at least) to bear witness to patient faith which endures suffering. As David Watson put it: 'James talks of the "patience of Job". We need to beware of an over-simplification in the realm of healing – "If you have faith you will be well." It is not always quite so straightforward as that.'

(b) We should not be gullible. Dr Peter May, a Christian GP, systematically investigates healing 'miracles'. He remains unconvinced. In his view, most (perhaps all) reports of modern healing miracles can – and should – be explained in natural medical terms. (You may wish to discuss his views later.)

(c) The gifts of the Spirit (see 1 Cor. 12–14; Eph. 4: 11–13; Rom. 12:6–8; and 1 Pet. 4: 10–11) include striking *and* unspectacular gifts. It is God's Spirit who enables helpers, administrators, encouragers and givers to be effective within the body of Christ.

> They (gifts of the Spirit) are never all given to one individual. They may – like healing powers or speaking in tongues – be quite extraordinary and even spectacular in nature. But they can also be almost secular, everyday capabilities, up to the point of good cash administration of a parish or community. (*Karl Rahner.*)

7. THE SPIRIT BRINGS POWER. Before his ascension, the risen Lord instructed his disciples to wait in Jerusalem. With the command he gave a promise (how often instructions and promises go together in the Bible): 'You will receive power when the Holy Spirit comes on you . . .'

Notice that the promise of power had a purpose in view. '. . . and you will be my witnesses' (Acts 1:8). The Holy Spirit was not given simply that they might *feel* good, but that they might *do* good.

The Greek word for power is *dunamis* – from which we get words like dynamic and dynamite. This is explosive stuff! But power isn't always exerted with a mighty bang. Last week I noticed a cracked path. It had been split open by a small plant which exerted gentle, persistent pressure over many weeks.

Both pictures – sticks of dynamite and the growing plant – illustrate the way God exerts his power in our lives and in our world. This power is given:

(a) to strengthen us in our struggle against temptation, wickedness and injustice.
(b) to enable us to witness to Jesus as Saviour, Lord and Friend.

8. THE SPIRIT BRINGS ASSURANCE. St Paul writes, 'Having believed, you were marked in him with a seal, the promised Holy Spirit, who is a deposit guaranteeing our inheritance' (Eph. 1:13–14). A famous hymn picks this up:

> Blessed assurance – Jesus is mine!
> Oh what a foretaste of glory divine!

Some Christians revel in this; others are much less enthusiastic. To them, it seems so arrogant. But those who sing this hymn with gusto are declaring their faith *in Jesus*, not in themselves. He is the one who receives sinners, gives promises to the faint-hearted, and throws wide open the gates of glory. Perhaps it is arrogant *not* to believe.

Of course, Christian 'certainty' can breed a kind of arrogance. True, 'there is now no condemnation for those who are in Christ Jesus' (Rom. 8:1). But with St Paul we must remember that we have not yet arrived. Like him, we must 'press on' (Phil. 3:14).

Some Christians live with no assurance at all. They read the Bible with psychological blinkers on. It is the tough aspects which get through; the gentle voice of God is never heard. Such Christians sometimes think that they have committed the sin against the Holy Spirit (Matt. 12.31–32). They feel that they are beyond God's love.

The very fact that they fear this shows they have nothing to fear! For 'the unforgivable sin' shows itself in pride, hardness of heart and a total unconcern for small matters like heaven and hell. If this paragraph describes you, God's Word says 'REPENT!' If the previous paragraph describes you, God's Word says 'RELAX!' Consider the unworthiness of the first disciples; remember that Jesus is the friend of sinners; rejoice that God is gracious, kind and long-suffering.

9. THE SPIRIT SOMETIMES STARTLES. I know a Christian businessman who often travels by train. He is an outgoing person who looks for opportunities to share his faith as he travels. One morning he 'heard' God's Spirit telling him to take a particular book on his journey.

He sat near a Chinese couple and he was aware that the woman was staring at his book. Eventually she played 'Snap' and produced an identical copy. They started talking and she requested prayer. Terry prayed in tongues; and then it was the turn of the man to stare: 'Where did you learn Chinese?' he demanded.

My friend does not know a word of Chinese. But according to the Chinese traveller, he was praying in fluent Mandarin! The train stopped outside Leeds station for half an hour and this enabled the conversation to develop. During this time Terry prayed with the visitor, who committed his life to Christ.

If you find this hard to believe – so do I! Stories like this usually come from 'a friend of a friend of a friend'. But here was a sane, honest friend describing his own extraordinary experience.

This incident underlines an important truth. The Spirit is sovereign. Jesus reminds us that we cannot control God's Spirit any more than we can control the wind (John 3:8). He is Sovereign Lord. Sometimes he works gently: sometimes he works with startling power. Our God is the living God – the God of surprises.

But it would be wrong to link the Holy Spirit too firmly with emotions, feelings and startling experiences. He is the *Spirit of Truth*. God's Spirit is concerned with straight thinking, deeper understanding and enlarged vision, as well as with warm hearts and joyful worship. To achieve this he often works steadily – but sometimes he needs to give us a sharp jolt.

10. THE SPIRIT BRINGS TROUBLE. . . . in two senses:
(a) He is the *Holy* Spirit. Jesus made it crystal clear that there is nothing complicated about receiving God's Spirit. We may find it helpful to ask other Christians to pray with us – with laying on of hands, perhaps. This can be done formally in Confirmation or informally at home. But we don't need to go through any special procedures. All we need is *to want* and *to ask*. 'If you then, though you are evil, know how to give good gifts to your children,

how much more will your Father in heaven give the Holy Spirit to those who ask him!' (Luke 11:13).

> If we invite the Spirit into our lives he *will* come. He may come gently – almost unnoticed at first – or he may come like a mighty wind. But come he will. That is the promise of Jesus, who does not break his word.

But he will come as a restless guest, not as a quiet, tame visitor. We have invited the *Holy* Spirit. He will put his finger on areas of our lives which we have not submitted to God's will. He wants to transform us into a living temple.

In some translations, the Holy Spirit is called 'the Comforter': the one who strengthens (John 14:16,26). This word can mislead, for the old usage is very different from our modern understanding. This is amusingly illustrated in one scene from the Bayeux Tapestry. It carries the caption 'King William comforteth his soldiers'. But we do not find the king with his arms around his men. No. He is prodding them into battle with his sword!

(b) The Spirit can be as troublesome within the Church as within individuals. New life can disturb old and settled customs. But sometimes the trouble caused in his name, is not really his doing.

This was true of the Church in Corinth. The Spirit brought new life, new gifts, new energy. But some church members claimed to be speaking and acting under the prompting of the Spirit, when they were doing no such thing. In reality, they were motivated by a desire for self-importance. St Paul spent a lot of time dealing with that, and trying to get the balance right. (1 Cor. 12–14).

11. THE SPIRIT PRAYS FOR US   Most Christians find prayer difficult – some of the time at least. In his love, God has given us his Spirit for this very reason. Consider this amazing promise: 'the Spirit helps us in our weakness. We do not know what we ought to pray for, but the Spirit himself intercedes for us with groans that words cannot express' (Rom. 8:26).

Our prayers may seem to be very inadequate. So they are. But God the Father hears not only *our* words. He also hears the Spirit as he prays for us.

The little boy in the Gospel story offered Jesus his packed lunch: two small fish and five loaves. The Lord took these, gave thanks, and multiplied them. He works in just the same way today, with anything that we offer him. In heaven we will be amazed at what God did with our prayers. For as we stumble and lose concentration, God's Holy Spirit prays in us and through us, with great and glorious fluency – and with enormous effectiveness.

CORE QUESTIONS . . .

For Group Discussion and Individual Reflection

1. 'There are those who worship the Father, the Son and the Virgin Mary; those who believe in the Father, the Son and the Holy Scriptures; those who found their faith on the Father, the Son and the Church; and there are even those who seem to derive their spiritual power from the Father, the Son and the minister!' (Dorothy L. Sayers).

   Dorothy Sayers suggests that, in reality, many Christians believe in a Binity rather than a Trinity! Do you? Zip through the following checklist individually.

(a) Do you ever pray to the Holy Spirit?   Yes/No

(b) Do you enjoy singing hymns to the Holy Spirit? (e.g. 'Come Holy Ghost'; 'Come Down O Love Divine'; 'Breathe On Me, Breath of God'.)   Yes/No

(c) Do you like your worship cool and controlled?   Yes/No

(d) Do you like your worship hot and exciting?   Yes/No

(e) Do you like your worship to be a mixture of (c) and (d)?   Yes/No

(f) Are you excited by, uneasy with, or sceptical about the train experience on Page 155?   ....

(g) Are you excited by, uneasy with, or sceptical about the healing miracle on Page 151–2?   ....

(h) Do you identify with the reservations expressed by Dr Peter May on Page 153?   Yes/No

(i) Can you recount similar experiences (your own or other people's)?   Yes/No

(j) Most Churches pray for the sick. Do you really expect to see results?   Yes/No

If working in a group, compare your answers to question 1 and discuss at leisure.

2. Do you feel that the thrust of the previous questions is wrong? Do you locate the Holy Spirit mainly in personal qualities such as love, joy and peace, rather than in remarkable manifestations such as healing and speaking in tongues?

3. Over the past twenty years many Christians and Churches have 'come alive in the Spirit' as a result of the charismatic movement. 'Renewal' has become a key word; worship has been transformed. Do members of your group have *good* experiences to share arising from this?

4. Inevitably – as in Corinth in New Testament times – new life brings new problems. Some people go too far and emphasise the wrong things. Do members of your group have *bad* experiences arising from this stress on the work of the Holy Spirit within the Church?

5. 'Every time that a man has, with a pure heart called upon Osiris, Dionysus, Krishna, Buddha, the Tao, etc., the Son of God has answered him by sending the Holy Spirit. And the Holy Spirit has acted upon his soul, not by inciting him to abandon his religious tradition, but by bestowing upon him light – and in the best of cases the fulness of light – in the heart of that same religious tradition' (Simone Weil).

   (a) Plenty to discuss here! Do you agree/disagree with Simone Weil?
   (b) Does the Holy Spirit inspire all musicians, artists and writers – or is his work only to do with holiness and the Church?

(c) What do you understand by John 16:13, 'But when he, the Spirit of truth, comes, he will guide you into all truth'?

BIBLE STUDY   Read Rom. 12:1–16 and 1 Cor. 12:7–11. No one possesses all the gifts of the Spirit – God scatters them around. But it remains true that we are told to 'eagerly desire' these gifts. So we need not be passive; we can (should?) pray and ask.

(a) Do you?
(b) Are there some gifts which make you nervous and which you do *not* want? Why?
(c) Which gift(s) of the Spirit do you think you possess?
(d) Which gifts do you think other members possess? (Only to be tackled in supportive groups!)
(e) Do you think such gifts are freely available today – or were they only for Bible times?

. . . AND MORE QUESTIONS

6. Harry Williams is an Anglican monk (irrelevant fact: he was Prince Charles' tutor at Cambridge). Discuss his words on Page 150. Are they true for you?

7. Put on the full armour of God . . . for our struggle is not against flesh and blood . . . And pray in the Spirit on all occasions (Eph. 6:11,12,18).

> Onward, Christian soldiers,
> Marching as to war . . .

What do you understand by the above? Are you aware of being in a spiritual battle?

8. John Richards recently wrote a book entitled *The Question of Healing Services* (DLT 1989). He writes from a charismatic position and has seen God do

mighty things. But his general approach is low key. He is worried that the current emphasis on 'signs and wonders' appears to locate God only in the extraordinary.

God *is* in the extraordinary of course; but he is in the *ordinary* stuff of our lives too. Can you share experiences of God in the *ordinary* (friendship, generosity, caring) — and in the *extraordinary* (healing; hearing God speak; remarkable guidance; words of knowledge)?

9. In the New Testament, the Holy Spirit is another term for the Spirit of Jesus — so Pentecost is closely linked with Easter. Do you have an 'unshakeable sense of being accompanied through life' by the risen Lord? If so:

   (a) Does he bring comfort, strength, understanding?
   (b) Does he bring challenge and discomfort? How? Be as specific as possible.
   (c) 'Do not grieve the Holy Spirit' (Eph. 4:30). Discuss.

10. (a) Do you feel that some people overdo Christian enthusiasm? Is this perhaps better than *under*doing it?
    (b) Have you ever attended a service or meeting which has embarrassed or frightened you? In what way?

11. 'You must be born again' said Jesus (John 3). The term means 'born from above'; born of God's Spirit.

   I heard a Christian dividing believers into two camps: those with a sudden conversion experience — and the rest. To distinguish the two she described the first group as 'born-again Christians'. She was rebuked by someone else who maintained that *all* Christians are born again, by definition. Views please.

12. Some Christians talk about 'being baptised in the Spirit'. They sometimes give the impression that this is an essential gateway to Christian progress and to a new and richer experience of God (Mk. 1:8; 1 Cor. 12:13)

   (a) Have you heard people talk like this?
   (b) What do you understand by it?
   (c) Does it encourage you?
   (d) Does it worry you?

   Note. Some *Viewpoints* touch on this. Michael Green discusses the issue in his fine book *I Believe in The Holy Spirit* (Hodder: revised 1985).

Homework?

(a) Write a prayer to the Holy Spirit.
(b) Take a well known tune and compose a hymn to the Holy Spirit.

BIBLE STUDY

(a) Try to recall the list of marvellous qualities in Galatians 5:22–23 (the fruit of the Spirit).
(b) Look up these verses to see how effective your memory is!
(c) Spend a few minutes trying to commit these nine key words to memory. Why not test one another?
(d) Perhaps the most surprising quality in this list is the last. God's Spirit helps us to exercise *self*-control. I have heard new Christians speak of God giving them strength to exercise self-control, where it was absent

before e.g. over swearing, wrong sexual practices, excessive drinking, bad temper . . . Will group members dare to share their successes – and their failures!

VIEWPOINTS

· **DAVID WATSON**   How, then, can a Christian be filled with the Spirit? The answer can be summarised in four words: Repent, Obey, Thirst, Ask.

· **BILLY GRAHAM**   The Bible teaches that the Holy Spirit is like the wind, and who can tell what the wind can do? Another symbol is the dove, and who can tell a dove when it can fly into the sky and what way to go? Water – living water, that shall be poured out in a mighty torrent – all these symbols express the sovereignty of God.

· **LORD COGGAN**   How very alarming! Nature's two most devastating agents, wind and fire. Have you ever been in the path of a hurricane? Have you ever seen a beautiful structure razed by fire? If you have, you will not easily sentimentalise about these elements.

· **E. STANLEY JONES**   The Church has in large measure tried to by-pass Pentecost . . . Had the disciples tried to by-pass Pentecost we would never have heard of them!

· **DR ROY POINTER**   What are the gifts of the Spirit? Specific attributes and abilities given to the people of God, in order that they might do the work of God, in the energy of the Spirit of God. The exercise of them will do at least two things: God will be glorified; the Church will be edified.

· **BLAISE PASCAL**   Fire . . . Certitude . . . Peace . . . joy, tears of joy.

- MICHAEL GREEN Thus, while baptism in the Spirit is the initial experience of Christ brought about by the Spirit in response to repentance, faith and baptism, the fulness of the Holy Spirit is intended to be the continual state of the Christian. It is not a plateau on to which you are ushered by some second stage in initiation, a plateau which separates you from other Christians who have not had the same experience. The New Testament gives no support to that view whatsoever.

- JOHN WIMBER How do we experience Spirit baptism? It comes at conversion . . . The born-again experience is the consummate charismatic experience . . . Having the Holy Spirit, however, does not guarantee that we will experience his power and gifts. More is required of us for that to happen. Paul even *commands* us to be filled with the Spirit.

- JOHN STOTT So the baptism of the Spirit in this verse (1 Cor. 12:13) far from being a dividing factor (some have it, others have not), is the great uniting factor (an experience we have all had).

- DAVID WATSON The balance here is so important. The devil is always trying to lead us off from our main task. If he can make the gifts of the Spirit the central theme in someone's message and ministry, he has won a strategic battle. 'Christ crucified and risen' – this is God's power for salvation.

- LORD RAMSEY It is often in groups of Christians meeting for prayer that a new openness to the Spirit is discovered. It is in such groups that it is vividly realised that the prayer of Christians is not of their own strength or initiative; the Spirit prays within them and they participate in the Spirit's prayer.

- **TOM SMAIL**　The coming of the Spirit takes place when people are together and it results in new relationships with God and with fellow Christians.

- **SPRING HARVEST EXECUTIVE**　Christians need an on-going and developing relationship with the Holy Spirit . . . it is possible to grieve the Holy Spirit by resisting his operation within our lives.

- **WCC (91)**　Spirit of God. Renew the whole Creation.

- **DOCTRINE COMMISSION 1991**　We value the charismatic movement for all the undoubted good it has brought to the Church. Equally, we wish to affirm and support those whose experience . . . has been rather different . . . for the Spirit is the Spirit of order as well as of surprise.

MEDITATION AND PRAYER

The Holy Spirit is that power which opens eyes that are closed, hearts that are unaware and minds that shrink from too much reality. (*Bishop John V. Taylor*).

Ask different group members to look up the following passages. Then ask them to read aloud – leaving time for silent meditation between each.

(a) Luke 11:13. A simple promise.
(b) 1 Corinthians 3:16; 1 Corinthians 6:19–20. Two stunning statements.
(c) Ezekiel 37:1–14. A sensational prophecy.

Read aloud – or sing – a hymn to the Holy Spirit.

Send your Holy Spirit and pour into our hearts that most excellent gift of love (Collect: Pentecost 7).

THE HOLY CATHOLIC CHURCH

> 'You are Peter, and on this rock I will build my
> church, and the gates of Hades will not overcome it'
> (Matt. 16:18).
> 'In him all things hold together. And he is the head
> of the body, the church' (Col. 1:17, 18).

GETTING STARTED

A Welsh Vicar attempted to introduce 'Passing the Peace'
into the Holy Communion Service on the first Sunday in
his new parish. He went to one woman near the front to
shake hands. She backed away.

She did shake his hand on leaving the church however,
so he asked why she had refused to do so earlier.

'Vicar,' she said, fixing him with a straight look. 'I
come to Church to worship God – not to be friendly.'

* * *

In *Screwtape Letters* (a Fount Paperback) C. S. Lewis sets
out an imaginary series of letters in which a senior devil
advises a junior tempter. The tempter is assigned to a man
who has recently come to faith in Christ:

> One of our great allies at present is the Church itself.
> Do not misunderstand me. I do not mean the Church as
> we see her spread out through all time and space and
> rooted in eternity, terrible as an army with banners.
> That, I confess, is a spectacle which makes our boldest

tempters uneasy. But fortunately it is quite invisible to
these humans . . .

When he gets to his pew and looks round him he sees
just that selection of his neighbours whom he has
hitherto avoided. You want to lean pretty heavily on
those neighbours. Make his mind flit to and fro between an expression like 'the body of Christ' and the
actual faces in the next pew. It matters very little, of
course, what kind of people that next pew really
contains. You may know one of them to be a great
warrior on the Enemy's side. No matter. Your patient,
thanks to Our Father below, is a fool. Provided that any
of those neighbours sing out of tune, or have boots that
squeak, or double chins, or odd clothes, the patient
will quite easily believe that their religion must therefore be somehow ridiculous.'

* * *

In *Miracle on the River Kwai* (Collins 1963) Ernest Gordon describes how he and many others rediscovered
Christianity in Japanese prisoner-of-war camps.

The Church was a fellowship of those who came in
freedom and love to acknowledge their weakness, to seek
a presence, and to pray for their fellows.

The confession of Jesus Christ as Lord was the one
requirement for membership . . . Two Chinese were
among those baptised. Some British troops had found
them still alive after a massacre . . . they were so impressed by what they had seen and heard of the example
of their Christian fellows that they asked to be admitted to
the Christian faith. So far as many of us could see, there
were three definitions of the Church.

There was the Church composed of laws, practices, pews, pulpits, stones and steeples; the Church adorned with the paraphernalia of State. Then there was the Church composed of creeds and catechisms, where it was identified only by words.

Finally there was the Church of the Spirit, called out of the world to exist in it by reason of its joyful response to the initiative of God's love. Such a Church had the atmosphere not of law court nor of class-room but of divine humanity. It existed wherever Christ's love burned in the heart of man. The physical temple and the doctrinal affirmation are both necessary to the fullness of the Church – but both are dead without the Church that is communion, the fellowship of God's people.

Ours was the Church of the Spirit . . . It was the throbbing heart of the camp – giving life to it, and transforming it from a mass of individuals into a community.

SETTING IT OUT

THE CATHOLIC CHURCH? A young couple came to church to hear their banns. We said the Apostles' Creed and they were puzzled. 'We thought this was the Church of England,' they said afterwards. 'So why did we say, "I believe in the Holy Catholic Church?"' To them 'Catholic' meant 'Roman Catholic'.

Not so. 'Catholic' means universal. So when we use this word in the Creed, we are asserting our fellowship with all Christians everywhere. The local Church is vitally important; but it is not the total Church. So it is our duty to pray for Christians in every corner of the world. And it is our joy to know that Christians right around the world are praying for us.

Archbishop William Temple spoke of this 'great new fact of our time'. He was referring to the glorious truth that in our century there is no continent – and virtually no country – without a Christian Church (however small) and some Christian witness (however fragile).

Of course, different cultures express their faith – and especially their worship – in different ways. But we have much in common, including the great Bible themes which are read and preached Sunday by Sunday.

This sense of oneness goes back to the earliest days. The Church in Jerusalem suffered during a famine and Paul put great energy into famine relief. The apostle mobilised Christians everywhere. He could do no other, for they were brothers and sisters – members of a common family, with God as their heavenly Father. So support for missionaries, Christian Aid, Tear Fund, and the Church Urban Fund is not an optional extra. Nor is *receiving* support, advice and encouragement from Christians overseas. These things are at the heart and centre of our common life in Christ.

A HOLY CHURCH?   That word 'holy' is perhaps the hardest single word in the entire Creed. Imagine a stranger coming to a Communion Service. He is from Japan and he knows something about Jesus – but very little about the Church. He notices that the people call the Church (i.e. themselves), 'holy'. Later, he hears the President declare, 'We are the body of Christ.' He may well be horrified. 'How *dare* you call yourselves holy? How *dare* you call yourselves the body of Christ?'

How indeed! We should certainly not do so without the highest authority to support us. But there it is in the New Testament: 'You are a royal priesthood, a holy nation' (1 Pet. 2:9). 'You are the body of Christ,' (1 Cor. 12:27).

If that visitor were to stay, his indignation would disappear. For he would note that the very people who make such incredible claims for themselves, also make statements of deep humility. They confess their sins; they admit that they are not worthy even to gather crumbs from under the Lord's Table.

Here is a glorious paradox. In the Bible, the Church is described in these incredibly high terms but it is not idealised. Indeed, many of the twenty-one New Testament letters were written in response to problems.

> The Bible represents the Church as it is: a group of wayward, short-sighted, squabbling human beings. But such is the grace, the power and the transforming love of God that it can be called a holy people, a royal priesthood, the body and bride of Christ, the Temple of the living God.

As members of the Church, we understand all too well what we *don't* mean by using these phrases. But we accept them in humility, and by God's grace we seek 'to become what we are'.

PROBING THE MEANING

Did Jesus Found the Church?

Think of Jesus walking from small town to even smaller village with his little band of disciples. Hold that picture in your mind. The dust; the sweat; the *simplicity* of it all. Then switch in your imagination to the most ornate

Church service that you can imagine. A vast building; a beautiful choir; magnificent robes; golden vessels.

Can there *really* be a connection between these two points?

Yes!

That connection is Jesus himself: for Jesus founded a community to embody his nature and carry on his work. We shall consider eight features:

(a) JESUS FOUNDED A COMMUNITY   From the beginning, Jesus called disciples to be with him. He called them in ones and twos but he insisted that they relate *to one another* as well as to him. It is clear that they didn't always find this easy. The saying that we choose our friends but not our relatives, applies here.

Our Christian brothers and sisters are not ours to choose; they are God's choice for us. Like it or not – *these* are the people with whom we hold a common faith. These are the people with whom we must weep, rejoice and share.

(b) JESUS FOUNDED A SACRAMENTAL COMMUNITY   At the Last Supper Jesus broke bread and spoke these startling words, 'Take and eat; this is my body.' Then he poured wine and said, 'Drink from it, all of you. This is my blood of the covenant, which is poured out for many for the forgiveness of sins' (Matt. 26:26–28).

Ever since, his disciples have followed that instruction.

Preferences vary. Some try to recapture the simplicity of a fellowship meal. Others emphasise the enormous significance of Jesus and his death for us, with ornate, highly-polished worship. Some express their joy in spontaneity, exuberance and clapping. Others (the Quakers) see every meal as a sacrament of grace. Yet others seek to honour Christ with beautiful note-perfect music.

Whatever the form, bread is broken, wine is poured and the Lord is remembered. Not as a dead hero. Not only as an inspiring teacher. But as the living Lord who welcomes us to *his* table. 'Christianity does not live on nostalgia, but celebrates a presence' (Leonardo Boff).

As the Church of England Rite A Holy Communion Service puts it:

President: 'The Lord is here.'
People: 'His Spirit is with us.'

(c) JESUS FOUNDED A LOVING COMMUNITY 'I give you a new commandment: love one another; as I have loved you, so you are to love one another' (John 13:34 REB). At first sight this is puzzling, for the command to love is not at all new. It is there in the Old Testament. Indeed, Jesus took two verses from the ancient Hebrew Scriptures to summarise the entire law and prophets.

Love your neighbour as yourself (Lev. 19:18).

\+

Love the Lord your God . . . with all your heart (Deut. 11:13).

\=

'"Love the Lord your God with all your heart and with all your soul and with all your mind." This is the first and greatest commandment. And the second is like it: "Love your neighbour as yourself." All the Law and the Prophets hang on these two commandments' (Matt. 22:37–40).

174 KNOW YOUR FAITH

So what is new about this commandment of Jesus? *Answer*: the phrase, 'as I have loved you'. His love is so great that 'he lay down his life for his friends' (John 15:13). So his call to love has sometimes involved literal martyrdom. 'The blood of the martyrs is the seed of the Church' as Tertullian so graphically put it in the second century.

Maximilian Kolbe was a Polish Franciscan priest who was captured by the Nazis. In the infamous concentration camp at Auschwitz, his dignity and faith sustained many of his fellow-sufferers.

Because of an attempted escape, some prisoners were condemned to death by starvation. One victim – a sergeant called Francis Gajowniczek – was very distressed. He had a wife and children, so Maximilian volunteered to change places.

The guard agreed to this grisly act of barter. The married man was spared; Fr Kolbe was locked away in Cell 18 without food. Two weeks later all were dead except four men; only Maximilian was fully conscious. On 14th August 1941 he was given phenol poison. He was forty-seven. On 14th August 1982 Maximilian was Canonised by the Polish Pope John Paul II, in the presence of the man whose life he had saved.

Few of us will be called to such an extravagant act of loving sacrifice. But the Bible caters for us too. Before he died on the cross, Jesus washed his disciples' feet. The New Testament is shot through with many gentle 'domestic' aspects of love, as well as great heroic acts.

'Therefore, as God's chosen people, holy and dearly loved, clothe yourselves with compassion, kindness, humility, gentleness and patience. Bear with each other and forgive whatever grievances you may have against one another. Forgive as the Lord forgave you. And over all these virtues put on love, which binds them all together in perfect unity' (Col. 3:12–14).

(d) JESUS SET HIS COMMUNITY IN THE WORLD   Some religious groups in Jesus' day sought to escape from the world. The most famous of these was the community which produced the Dead Sea Scrolls – the Essene Community at Qumran on the Dead Sea.

But this was not the way of Jesus. He looked at that unlikely bunch of early disciples and he spoke amazing words. Not, you will *become* the light of the world; but – you *are* the light of the world. Not, you are to be the salt of the earth; but – you *are* the salt of the earth. Salt was used to prevent food from rotting in those days before refrigeration. And it added flavour and zest to an unvaried diet.

Despite 2,000 years of failure within the Church, these titles still apply. We rejoice at recent events in Eastern Europe – and we recall that in many of those countries the Church played a unique role in keeping the flame of freedom and hope alight. Looking further afield, we can be proud of the Base Communities, made up of the poorest people in South America. And we can ponder the fact that it is hard to find a significant caring agency in Britain which does not have a substantial Christian input.

This applies to ancient foundations like hospitals, schools and universities. It applies to Victorian foundations like Children's Homes (e.g. Barnardos). And it applies to more recent organisations too. Samaritans was started by a London rector. Shelter was formed by the coming together of five housing agencies, three of which contained the word Christian or Church or Catholic. Amnesty was founded by a young Christian lawyer and was born in prayer and fellowship. The Hospice Movement was pioneered by Christians.

The Observer (18/3/90) carried a moving article about an uneducated prisoner who came alive intellectually on discovering the poetry of T. S. Eliot. He wrote about his attempt to pick up the threads of life on his release. In a throwaway line, he adds that he was received and welcomed into his local Church by non-judgemental people.

I started going to Church a bit, and I found at our local one they had quite a big social group of people round about my own age, in their early thirties . . . I'd told the group my story soon after I joined. None of them turned their backs on me.

No one who knows the Church from the inside is likely to be starry-eyed about the Church's success in following its calling to be salt and light. There are many painful failures. But I am with Jim Wallis (founder of the Sojourners' Community in Washington), when he says that he cannot think of a more supportive place to be, in bad times or good, than in the Church of Jesus Christ.

(e) JESUS FOUNDED A COMMUNITY WHICH BEARS HIS NAME In the accounts of the famous Damascus Road experience of St Paul, we find a significant phrase. Jesus' voice from heaven asks a pointed question: 'Saul, Saul why do you persecute me?' Jesus is so closely identified with his people, that to persecute *them* is to persecute *him*.

Hence that dazzling phrase, 'The Body of Christ'. The Incarnation must go on. But how? By the Spirit of Jesus working through the family of Jesus.

A black boy was amazed when a white priest raised his hat to his mother. In South Africa, white men didn't do such things to black women. That teenager was even more impressed when that same priest visited him regularly throughout his long spell in hospital. The priest's love, humility and care were important factors in the decision of that boy to offer himself for ordination and Christian leadership. The white man was Trevor Huddleston; the black boy was Desmond Tutu.

(f) JESUS FOUNDED A COLOURBLIND COMMUNITY A story is told about George Thomas, the former Speaker of the House of Commons and Methodist lay preacher. He went to America and was invited to preach in an all-white Church. He was hesitant but agreed to do so provided he could preach in a black Church too. This was arranged and he preached with typical Welsh fervour. At the end of the service, a black Christian expressed his gratitude. He went on to say, 'Mr Thomas, your skin may be white but your heart's *real* black.'

If that story isn't true, then it ought to be! George Thomas' insistence is in line with New Testament teaching: 'There is neither Jew nor Greek, slave nor free, male nor female, for you are all one in Christ Jesus' (Gal. 3:28). The early Christians discovered the astounding truth that Jesus had knocked down every wall of partition between races and social classes. They had no political means of attacking the institution of slavery. But they undermined it, by insisting that slaves and slave-owners were brothers and sisters.

> The Christian attitude to slavery placed an explosive charge under the entire institution. (*Professor C. F. D. Moule.*)

(g) JESUS FOUNDED AN APOSTOLIC COMMUNITY   'Go and tell,' said the risen Lord to the two Marys. 'Make disciples of all nations' was his final command to the disciples. Those words come down to us across the centuries. The noun 'apostle' comes from the verb 'to send'. The Church is not allowed to hug the Gospel to itself. Good News is for sharing – which is, in itself, an act of loving service. We are a missionary Church or we are nothing.

In the 1990's, many Churches are taking this responsibility very seriously. Believers from all styles of churchmanship have declared their intention to 'make Christ known' in a decade of evangelism.

> The one and only essential commission which the Church has been given with regard to the world is to be a witness to the world. (*Hans Küng.*)

An apostolic community suggests a growing community. Europe is a tough mission field and the Church is struggling, as the *English Church Census (1991)* shows. But there are still 3.7 million adult Christian worshippers in England, there are many growing Churches even here, and the Church in some parts of the world is expanding rapidly. Complacency would be absurd. But we are – or should be – in good heart.

(h) JESUS FOUNDED AN ETERNAL COMMUNITY 'I will not drink again of the fruit of the vine until that day when I drink it anew in the Kingdom of God' (Mark 14:25). Jesus was referring to the wine which he shared with his disciples at the Last Supper. He made it clear:

· that life would go on beyond the grave

· that it would be a life of fellowship

This great truth is reinforced by an earlier phrase in the Creed: 'I believe in the resurrection of the body.' The life of heaven is solid, real and glorious. Compared with that, our lives on earth are like shadow compared with substance. In other words, those who die 'in the Lord' are more living than the living. They are in fellowship with one another, as they join with the music of heaven in praise and worship directed to 'the Lamb upon the Throne'. Though unseen, they are united with us, and we with them. Together we worship 'with angels and archangels and all the company of heaven'.

As we face bereavement and observe ourselves growing older, this is a great comfort. It is a great challenge too. 'Since we are surrounded by such a great cloud of witnesses,' writes the anonymous author of the letter to the Hebrews, 'let us throw off everything that hinders and the sin that so easily entangles' (Heb. 12:1).

I used to think that verse described an arena, with the saints in heaven witnessing *us* – watching us and cheering us on. Perhaps they do. But the verse doesn't say this. It refers to *their* witness to faith in the living God, not ours. Consider Jesus, says the writer. And think of those who put their faith in God in past generations. Let their lives be a challenge and an inspiration. We joyfully assent to this when we say, 'I believe in the Communion of Saints.'

In popular usage the word 'saint' refers to a well-known hero of the faith. But in the New Testament, 'saints' is used to describe ordinary Christians. It is related to the word 'holy' and it means 'set apart' – set apart by God to serve him in the world. This applies to every believer, not just a select group. So while the Church canonises a few, the New Testament makes saints of us all.

CORE QUESTIONS . . .

For Group Discussion and Individual Reflection

1. Do members of your group have a narrow or wide experience of Church worship? E.g. when on holiday do you:
   (a) Go to a Church similar to your own?
   (b) Experience something different (silence with the Quakers; mass with the Roman Catholics; beautiful music with the Orthodox; unpredictability with the Anglicans; clapping with the Pentecostals)?
   (c) Take a holiday from Church?

2. 'Make every effort to keep the unity of the Spirit through the bond of peace' (Eph. 4:3):
   (a) Do you have strong links with other Churches/Christian fellowships in your district?
   (b) Do you think this should be a priority – or are other things more important?
   (c) Given a free hand, how would you modify or extend these links?
   (d) Paul's words apply to unity *within* the local fellowship, as well as between Churches. How would you rate a sense of family unity within your Church on an A to E scale? (A = excellent; E = poor).

3. If a stranger came to your Church, do you think (s)he would be:
   (a) Swamped by too many folk greeting him/her?
   (b) Ignored?
   (c) Made to feel welcome?
   (d) Made to sit at the front because regulars crowd at the back?
   (e) To test your views, why not ask a couple of friends (who are unknown to your fellow members) to attend and report back?
   (f) Do you think the reaction would be different if the person was a little 'different' e.g. handicapped, black, a punk?

4. 'I don't need to go to Church to be a Christian.' What would you say in answer to this not uncommon assertion?

5. I heard a man with a high-powered job say that he doesn't go to Church — because he meets people there whom he normally talks to only as the boss.
   One of the glories of many local Churches is their social mix. Solicitors and people on Income Support are on Christian-name terms, just as the New Testament encourages:
   (a) Is this true of your church?
   (b) Does this go far enough? Is it right for wealthy people to worship with poor people — with a clear conscience? Shouldn't the 'good things' be shared more equally? Are we *really* the family of God? If not; do you have solutions?

6. (a) 'The Church of England is dying of good taste' (Archbishop William Temple?). Is it?
   (b) Do you agree with 1, 2, 3 on page 15?

BIBLE STUDY Brainstorm your group for New Testament titles of the Church. How many can you produce? If stuck, look up 1 Corinthians 12:27; and 1 Peter 2:4–10.

    (a) Which means most to you personally?

    (b) The Church is described as 'the bride of Christ'. What do you understand by this? Is this particular title a problem for men in the Church?

    (c) In the New Testament the *whole church* is described as a 'royal priesthood' and Christian leaders are nowhere described as priests. Where does this leave the notion of the parish priest?

    (d) Should titles like Reverend, Very Reverend and Most Reverend have any place in the church of Jesus Christ? (Is Matt. 23:8–12 relevant?)

. . . AND MORE QUESTIONS

7. If you go about this country, from parish to parish, you will find parishes which seem lifeless: the worship is formal, the worshippers are like separate units . . . Go to others: there is true fellowship . . . there is an outgoing force in mission and service' (*Archbishop Michael Ramsey*).

    (a) Can your Church fairly be described as 'salt' and 'light' in your locality? Or does it exist mainly for the benefit of its members?

    (b) Would your district miss you if you closed down? If so, in what ways?

    (c) Whatever your answers to (a) and (b), do you have any ideas to make the words 'salt' and 'light' fit more closely? List five good points about your Church and five 'could do better' points. If you could make two changes to Church life (local, national or international) what would they be?

8. Conduct a survey among non Church-goers to get their answers to the previous questions? If 'survey' sounds too formal – ask a non Church-going friend or two *why* they don't attend and *what* (if anything) the Church could do to attract them. e.g.
   (a) Is the style of the Services right?
   (b) Is the timing of Services right?
   (c) Are your organisations appropriate/attractive?
   (d) Are your policies (e.g. baptism, marriage) sensitive and aware?
   (e) Does too much happen 'inside' rather than 'outside'?

9. (a) Is a sense of belonging to the universal Church important to you, or do you think largely in terms of your local Church? Do you feel you have the balance right?
   (b) Does your Church support Christians in other places – in Britain or abroad? Are you (as a Church or as an individual) supported by/linked with Christians elsewhere? If not, is this worth exploring?
   (c) Do you 'feel' (i.e. *within* yourself, not necessarily in physical terms like letters or gifts) any meaningful solidarity with the Church in Poland, South Africa – or any other country overseas? (See final meditation and prayer.)

10. *'I believe in the Communion of Saints.'* 'Therefore, since we are surrounded by such a great cloud of witnesses . . .' (Heb. 12:1).
    (a) Do you celebrate All Saints' Day? If so, how?

(b) If not – are you missing out?

(c) Is 'the Communion of Saints' an empty phrase for you – or is it full of meaning?

11. In its Liturgy the Church often refers to angels and archangels. But they are seldom heard of outside Church worship – even among Christians. Do they have a part to play in our lives? (I am grateful to Cardinal Suenens for this question.)

12. (a) Physical gestures tend to divide Christians! They enable us to 'pigeon-hole' our fellow believers:
Do you cross yourself, genuflect, raise your arms, dance . . .?

How do you feel when others do these things?

(b) I know people who refuse to attend a particular Church because incense is used. Are they being silly?

Is that Church being foolish in using an 'aid' to worship which divides Christians?

(c) Clergy in the York Diocese have been directed not to use Christian names when administering Communion. What do you think about this?

13. At the 1988 Lambeth Conference the Anglican Bishops defined the Mission of the Church under four headings.

(a) Write down your four headings before looking at the third Viewpoint on Page 185.

(b) Do you have ideas as to how your Church might attempt to tackle the first on the Bishops' list in a Decade of Evangelism? (Note: I have many practical suggestions. If you want these please send a note to me via CWN/the publishers: SAE please!)

VIEWPOINTS

- **ARCHBISHOP GEORGE CAREY**   There is of course a lot wrong with the Churches and we must not disguise our weakness and poverty.

- **JOHN WESLEY**   The Bible knows nothing of solitary religion.

- **THE LAMBETH CONFERENCE 1988**   The mission of the Church is:

  (1) to proclaim the Good News of the Kingdom;
  (2) to teach, baptise and nurture new believers;
  (3) to respond to human need by loving service;
  (4) to seek to transform unjust structures of society.

- **DR ROY POINTER**   That little old lady sitting at the back of your Church; she has a ministry and your Church is deficient if her ministry isn't exercised.

- **THOMAS MERTON**   The Church as a visible society has, of course, her organisation, laws and discipline. But these are all secondary, and relatively unimportant compared with the principle of inner and spiritual unity which is the charity of Christ.

- **LORD RAMSEY**   So the Church spans heaven and earth. What does the Church exist to do? It lives towards God, and towards the world. Towards God, it worships: towards the world it preaches the Gospel, it brings people into fellowship with God, it infects the world with righteousness, it speaks of divine principles on which the life of humanity is ordered. [Note: Lord Ramsey makes it clear that he is aware of the *other* side of this picture – divisions etc.]

- **A. C. SWINBURNE**   I could worship the crucified, if he came to me without his leprous bride, the Church.

- **PROFESSOR HANS KÜNG**   The real Church is not an ideal . . . floating somewhere between God and men. The real Church is rather the Church of God, composed of men, existing in the world for the world.

- **THE EMPEROR CHARLEMAGNE**   (Eighth century.) Any unbaptised Saxon who attempts to hide himself among his own people and refuses to accept baptism shall be put to death.

- **BILLY GRAHAM**   Christianity is a religion of fellowship. Following Christ means love, righteousness, service, and these can only be achieved and expressed through social relations.

- **MOTHER TERESA**   When Therese of Lisieux – the Little Flower – died and was about to be canonised, everyone was asking, 'What reason is there for the Holy Father to canonise her? She hasn't done anything extraordinary.' The Holy Father pointed out in writing the reason for his decision: 'I want to canonise her because she did ordinary things with extraordinary love.'

- **DIETRICH BONHOEFFER**   The first service that one owes to others in the fellowship consists in listening to them. Just as love for God begins with listening to his Word, so the beginning of love for our friends is learning to listen to them.

- **ANON**   We have 100 members in our church but 50 are very old – which leaves 50 to do the work. Of those 50, 25 are very busy – which leaves 25 to do the work. Of those 25, 13 are very tired which leaves 12 . . . (Complete the saga yourself!)

- **DAVID MAKEPEACE** To engage fully in the Mission of the Church we need to live out our faith in relationships which are characterised by transparency, honesty, reality and love.

- **CHRISTOPHER IDLE** The very words 'coming to church' or 'churchgoing' would be incomprehensible to the first Christians. 'Church' had two basic meanings; first the whole company of Christian believers (as in the Creed), second, the local congregation (as in the 39 Articles). The church meets in some special and much loved buildings, but when the last person out shuts the door, the church is no longer there!

- **JURGEN MOLTMANN** Without Christ, no Church . . . there is only a Church if and as long as Jesus of Nazareth is believed and acknowledged as the Christ of God.

- **FROM THE CHINESE CHURCH** If a Christian has never suffered, then he cannot understand God's blessing. He is like a child without training. (Pastor Samuel Lin, Canton.) We have more than a hundred people in our meeting but only one of them has a Bible. (Anhui Province 1990.)

- **ERNEST GORDON** (Writing about his experience of the Church in a prisoner-of-war-camp.) From the Church we received the inspiration that made life possible, the inbreathing of the Holy Spirit that enabled men to live better lives, to create improvements for the good of others, and to make kind neighbours. The fruits were in evidence around us: 'love, joy, peace, long-suffering, gentleness, goodness, and faith.'

- **ARCHBISHOP GEORGE CAREY** We cannot belong to Christ on our own; it is impossible to be a Robinson

Crusoe Christian. We need the human family in order to live and grow and similarly we need the Christian family to grow up as Christians.

MEDITATION AND PRAYER

I believe in Christianity as I believe the sun has risen not only because I see it, but because by it I see everything else (C. S. Lewis).

Adopt an attitude of prayer. Go round the world in your imagination, visiting a cathedral, a mud hut, a prison chapel, an open-air service . . . Then marvel and rejoice that you are part of this worldwide family which is still the biggest and most influential movement that the world has ever known. Re-read Archbishop Carey (above).

Almighty God,
who called your Church to witness
that you were in Christ reconciling men to yourself:
help us so to proclaim the good news of your love,
that all who hear it may be reconciled to you;
through him who died for us and rose again
and reigns with you and the Holy Spirit,
one God, now and for ever. (Collect: Pentecost 12)

Send us out in the power of your Spirit . . .

POSTSCRIPT

In the Bible, faith is dynamic. It never remains in the head; it affects the heart and the will. Faith moulds attitudes and character; it gives rise to purposeful action and quiet contentment. So it is appropriate to conclude a book entitled *Know Your Faith* with a simple but searching checklist.

* * *

My faith and . . . my inner life

> 'Be still, and know that I am God' (Ps. 46:10).

- Do I find a few minutes most days to reflect, to pray, to read the Scriptures?

> 'Cast all your anxiety on him' (1 Pet. 5:7).

- Do I relate my faith to life's problems and joys?

My faith and . . . my friendships and family

> 'Love is patient, love is kind' (1 Cor. 13:4).

- Am I helpful, encouraging, supportive?
- Am I demanding and irritable?
- Can I give and receive forgiveness?
- Am I generous? Can I accept generosity?

My faith and . . . the wider world

> 'I urge . . . that requests, prayers, intercession and thanksgiving be made . . . for all in authority' (1 Tim. 2:1).

- Are my concerns too local?

- Is my life too wrapped up in a small circle of friends?

- Am I willing to risk new situations?

- Do I relate my faith to the daily news?

My faith and . . . God

'Since we have been justified through faith, we have peace with God' (Rom. 5:1).

- Does my faith set me free or pile on more burdens?

- If my answers so far are depressing, will I turn to God and God's people for help?

- Do I heed the tough demands of Jesus?

- Do I enjoy his gentle words and glorious promises too?

- Is my faith based on rules or on a relationship with God?

* * *

'The only thing that counts is faith expressing itself through love' (Gal. 5:6).

'How can this strange story of God made man, of a crucified saviour, of resurrection and new creation, become credible for those whose entire mental training has conditioned them to believe that the real world is the world which can be satisfactorily explained and managed without the hypothesis of God? I know of only one clue to the answering of that question . . . a congregation which believes it . . .' (Bishop Lesslie Newbigin)